Nature Rx

Nature Rx

Improving College-Student Mental Health

Donald A. Rakow and Gregory T. Eells

Comstock Publishing Associates
An imprint of Cornell University Press

Ithaca and London

First published 2019 by Cornell University Press

Library of Congress Cataloging-in-Publication Data

Names: Rakow, Donald Andrew, 1951– author. | Eells, Gregory T., 1967– author.
Title: Nature Rx : improving college-student mental health / Donald A. Rakow
    and Gregory T. Eells.
Description: Ithaca [New York] : Comstock Publishing Associates, an imprint of
    Cornell University Press, 2019. | Includes bibliographical references and index.
Identifiers: LCCN 2018052242 (print) | LCCN 2018052970 (ebook) |
    ISBN 9781501715297 (e-book epub/mobi) | ISBN 9781501715303 (e-book pdf) |
    ISBN 9781501715280 | ISBN 9781501715280 (pbk.)
Subjects: LCSH: College students—Mental health—United States. | Nature—
    Psychological aspects. | Outdoor recreation—Psychological aspects. | Nature,
    Healing power of.
Classification: LCC RC451.4.S7 (ebook) | LCC RC451.4.S7 R35 2019 (print) |
    DDC 616.8900835—dc23
LC record available at https://lccn.loc.gov/2018052242

I would like to acknowledge the continued support of my wife, Michelle, and my three children, Kayla, Cole, and Cade. I would also like to acknowledge my incredible colleagues at CPS and Cornell Health.

—Greg Eells

I would like to thank my wife, Sue, who keeps me grounded; all my Cornell collaborators on the Nature Rx project; and nature itself, which inspires me every day.

—Don Rakow

Contents

Acknowledgments

We would like to thank the following college and university collaborators:

Kathleen Socolofsky, Carmia Feldman, Stacey Parker, and A. Haven Kiers from the UC Davis Arboretum and Public Garden

Jeannie Larson from the Minnesota Landscape Arboretum and the Earl E. Bakken Center for Spirituality & Healing at the University of Minnesota

Dorothy Ibes from the Parks Research Lab of the College of William and Mary

Members of the 2018 Nature Rx@Cornell Steering Committee: Catherine Thrasher-Carroll, David Cutter, Marianne Krasny, Marc Magnus-Sharpe, Kevin Moss, Philip Robinson, Naomi Sachs, Nancy Wells; interns Grace Robbins and Allyson LaRosa; and students Denisse Gayosso-Lucano, Lauren Yeaman, Kellie Damann, and Sarah Marino

Nature Rx

Introduction

In contemporary culture, we are increasingly disconnected from our roots in the natural world. The majority of us live in densely populated urban areas and spend more time in front of a screen than in the woods. Significant social changes have contributed to fewer people being intentionally engaged with nature. This increasing disconnection seems related to a growing number of physical and mental health concerns. Institutions of higher education (IHEs), the diverse collection of colleges and universities around the world, are in a unique position to develop programs to reverse this trend. In this book we will address how social changes are impacting the mental and physical health of students attending IHEs and look at some of the programs developed at different institutions. The book should be of interest to practitioners in campus counseling centers; staff in student life centers; faculty instructors in disciplines as diverse as psychology, landscape architecture, and environmental sciences; members of NASPA (Student Affairs Administrators in Higher Education) and the American College Health Association; and practitioners in the public garden field.

In chapter 1, we address the growing mental health crisis on US campuses, exploring the results of surveys that indicate rising levels of anxiety and depression in addition to other mental health concerns among student populations. We present data on the increasing number of students who are seeking professional help and offer an analysis of potential causes of this trend. The chapter concludes with a review of how IHEs are responding to the surging demand for mental health care, including different public health approaches that have been found to be effective on various IHE campuses. This broad public health approach provides the foundation for the development of programs that encourage students to spend time in nature as a response to mental health concerns.

In chapter 2 we explore the science behind the mental health benefits of spending more time in nature, specifically the ways in which such time improves concentration and reduces stress. This examination includes a review of attention restoration theory, developed by Rachel Kaplan and Stephen Kaplan in 1989, which outlines how restoration occurs when we are away from the norm, and how a natural area provides a sense of compatibility and discovery. This chapter also describes stress-reduction theory, proposed by Roger Ulrich and colleagues (1991), which focuses on how we respond to external stressors. The theory posits that responses occur through changes in the body's physiology. We then tie stress-reduction theory to the practice of forest bathing (*shinrin-yoku*), a mindfulness-based relaxation approach first popularized in Japan. Other approaches are also explored, including wilderness adventure experiences and their ability to build resilience. We conclude the chapter by discussing how gardening and interacting with the soil can strengthen the immune system. We also provide guidance around the question of the appropriate dosage of nature to have positive health impacts.

In chapter 3 we specifically address how to develop a Nature Rx program on a college campus, framing our discussion in the context of the national obesity epidemic and the public health need for individuals to become more physically active. The chapter traces the history of the DC Park Rx program and how physicians began prescribing time in nature. Our overview includes a look at the Park Rx America program, the Walk with a Doc program in Columbus, Ohio, and the LiveWell Greenville program in South Carolina. We then outline the steps that can be taken to start a Nature Rx program in a higher education environment. These include organizing a committed group with broad representation across campus, securing support among top administrators, inventorying available green spaces, engaging students, intentionally partnering with health and counseling services, developing easily usable apps and/or websites, cultivating relationships with relevant academic programs, developing an approach to effectively evaluate the program, identifying challenges, and modeling the desired behavior around time in nature.

In chapter 4 we outline Nature Rx programs on four university campuses, first acknowledging the significant impact the physical grounds of a campus can have on students or potential students. We then address the unique components of each program, identifying successes and challenges. Particular attention is given to the transferability of these programs to other campuses, large or small, rural or urban.

In the final chapter we address the potential role of Nature Rx programs in the future of higher education and explore the limitations and barriers to creating such programs. Examples of limitations are climate, geography, and the physical structures of individual institutions. We conclude the chapter with suggestions about how to measure the effectiveness of Nature Rx programs and their future potential to ameliorate the physical and mental health challenges found on campuses.

1

The Mental Health Crisis on US Campuses

Background

Over the past decade considerable attention has been given to the mental health and well-being of university students across the United States and in many other countries. This attention has often focused on the growing demand for mental health services, the perspectives of students and parents on unmet mental health needs, rising levels of anxiety and depression, and concerns about student suicide.[1] Common questions asked include "Are students experiencing increased levels of mental health concerns?" "Is there an increasing demand for mental health services?" "If there is an increase in mental health concerns, then what are the causes?" And last, "What are colleges and universities doing to respond to this landscape?"

In this chapter we will attempt to answer these questions by reviewing recent surveys of college students and counselors and clinical data from hundreds of college and university counseling services. We will then delve into a variety of theories about the underlying causes of psychological distress among college-aged youth and describe different efforts colleges and universities are making to address the demands through a public health approach and by providing effective mental health treatment, as well as by examining other ways—like encouraging more time in nature—to create a campus culture that supports student mental health.

Are Students Experiencing Increased Levels of Mental Health Concerns?

Clearly, students *are* experiencing increased levels of various mental health concerns. The 2015 American Freshmen Survey reported that the emotional health of incoming freshmen is at the lowest point in at least three decades.[2] The 2015 National Collegiate Health Assessment corroborated this assessment, finding that 37 percent of 116,468 college students surveyed felt so depressed within the previous twelve months that it was difficult for them to function, and 59 percent felt overwhelming anxiety.

To find a more nuanced answer to this question we can review the last six years of data from the Center for Collegiate Mental Health (CCMH). The CCMH was established in 2004 at Pennsylvania State University and describes itself as "an international Practice-Research-Network (PRN) that brings together clinical work, research, and technology. CCMH collects data through the routine clinical practices of over 350 college and university counseling centers internationally, creating the largest PRN of its kind. CCMH reports on over 100,000 unique clients annually."[3] The purpose of this innovative PRN is to create clinical tools, resources, and research through the data that is collected and to use the data to inform the clinical work done on college campuses as well as policies and practices. It is considered the best source of data on student clinical presentation and counseling service practice.

The CCMH *2016 Annual Report* presented anonymized data from 139 college and university counseling centers, describing

FIGURE 1-1
Student displaying stress
(Courtesy of Skorton Center for Health Initiatives, Cornell Health)

150,483 unique college students seeking mental health treatment, and representing 3,419 clinicians and over 1 million appointments. The CCMH found that over six years approximately half of all students seeking mental health care had already been in some type of therapy. They reported that nearly one-third of students seeking care have been on some type of psychotropic medication and one in ten have been hospitalized for psychiatric reasons. The stability of the data indicates that there is not an overall increase in preexisting mental health conditions.[4]

It is also important to examine which aspects of presenting mental health concerns are stable and which ones are showing increases. The CCMH measures mental health broadly through the use of the Counseling Center Assessment of Psychological Symptoms (CCAPS), which is a multidimensional assessment and outcome measure. The CCMH report shows a small but persistent increase in students' self-reported depression, generalized anxiety, social anxiety, and academic distress over the past six years. These conditions are also the most predominant concerns to counseling centers. However, other common presenting mental health concerns, such as eating disorders, hostility, substance use, and family distress, have remained relatively stable over the same six-year period. Though these concerns have not been increasing, their prevalence continues to persist at relatively high levels and often leads to students needing clinical support beyond a counseling service at a college or university.

Is There an Increasing Demand for Mental Health Services?

In the 2016 National Survey of College Counseling Services, 94 percent of Counseling and Psychological Services (CAPS) center directors indicated that the number of students with severe psychological problems continues to increase on their campuses. Meanwhile, 76.6 percent of college counseling directors reported that they had to reduce the number of visits for noncrisis patients to cope with the increasing overall number of clients.[5] Another finding that confirms the continuing demand for services comes from a supplemental survey of CCMH members that, in 2015, examined changes in institutional enrollment and counseling center utilization over the last six years (2009–10 through 2014–15). This survey found that, on average, the growth in the number of students seeking services at counseling centers was more than five times the rate of institutional enrollment growth. Additionally, the growth in counseling center appointments was more than seven times the rate of institutional enrollment growth. An important implication from this data is that there is a disproportionate impact on demand for counseling services as institutions increase their enrollment.

What Are the Causes of Increased Mental Health Concerns?

There are myriad theories about the growing mental health concerns and the concomitant increase in demand for mental health care. A general observation is that many students struggle with managing uncomfortable emotions and display low levels of distress tolerance. This trend may be related to increases in technology use and feelings of general isolation.[6] Various studies continue to point to the ubiquity and frequency of smartphone use and social media time being significant contributors to a variety of mental health concerns.[7]

Over the past fifteen years, a considerable number of large-scale interventions and intentional changes have been instituted at US universities that have led to a cumulative impact on their campuses. Many of the trends in students seeking care and utilizing more resources are the intended outcomes of these interventions. At a macro level one of the most influential changes was the signing into law in 2004 of the Garrett Lee Smith Memorial Act (GLSMA). The intent of this law was to reduce the incidence of suicide among college students by encouraging practitioners at IHEs (institutions of higher education) to take a public health approach. The passage of the GLSMA led to the investment of tens of millions of dollars to numerous IHEs. More specifically, the act worked to educate campus communities about mental health, reduce stigma around mental health issues, intentionally increase help seeking among students in need, and improve the ability of faculty, staff, and students to identify at-risk students and get them to appropriate help.

What Are Colleges and Universities Doing to Respond to This Landscape?

The passage of the GLSMA helped provide funding and a cultural shift for how IHEs began to respond to the changing landscape around mental health by taking a broad-based public health approach. This approach includes recognizing that multiple dimensions of the educational environment can influence individual health, such as aspects of the academic milieu, campus climate, social scene, available mental health care, and articulated community values in relation to mental health. Since these aspects of campus life can serve as both protective *and* risk factors, it is important to develop strategies for influencing them in the direction of health and well-being.

One of the first steps in addressing educational environment and climate issues is to begin with leadership commitment to these efforts. Such efforts are not a new development in the United States or internationally. As long ago as 1995, the University of Central Lancashire (UK) instituted a Health Promoting University project. After a university-wide review, it was agreed that the goals of this project should be:

- to integrate within the university's structures, processes, and culture a commitment to health and to developing its health-promoting potential; and
- to promote the health and well-being of staff, students, and the wider community.[8]

Such leadership commitment has been manifested at Cornell University through a video we developed and disseminated called *Real Students, Reel Stories* that is shown during a mandatory orientation program for all first-year undergraduates. In the video, current students, recent alumni, and the university president at the time David J. Skorton give advice to first-year students about adjusting to college life, including how to maintain perspective in the face of setbacks. Students are encouraged to consider their expectations, hearing older students tell them that although they all did well in high school, "not everyone gets all As at Cornell." President Skorton tells them that when he was in college, he failed a class . . . and became an Ivy League president nonetheless.

The University of Minnesota is another institution that recognized the importance of mental health issues to all aspects of campus life. Their Provost's Committee on Student Mental Health (PCSMH), created in 2005, brings together twenty-three members representing key campus offices, departments, and programs, along with undergraduate and graduate students from key student organizations, to raise awareness about issues related to student mental health, including ways to effect policy change, improve conditions on campus for students with mental health concerns, and serve as a model of collaboration for the campus and other universities.[9]

The University of North Carolina–Greensboro addresses these broader environmental issues by making effective use of their Spartan Experience Questionnaire. They use this local data in addition to national reports to determine areas of immediate or emerging concern as well as areas where targeted interventions have been successful. In addition to these efforts, data about campus health care, mental health care, assistance for students in distress, and student participation rates in campus recreation, club, and intramural sports are all shared in their *Division of Student Affairs Annual Report,* which is forwarded to decision makers and stakeholders. This constant cycle of evaluation and review ensures that health and wellness efforts meet students where they are and that the environment evolves to meet students' needs.[10]

Another component of this approach is to develop broad programming focused on fostering psychological resilience, the ability to "bounce back" from the external stressors that are inherent in life. There is increasing evidence that resilience is malleable and can be fostered through practices such as stress and time management, mindfulness meditation, and cognitive exercises that focus on optimism, a growth mind-set, and gratitude. Cornell offers a program called "Staying Balanced," which introduces students to these elements of resilience. Resilience also has a social dimension, with students who experience real or perceived isolation being at greater risk for distress compared to those who are connected to others at a personal level. Strategies that foster community building within our residential programs and efforts to encourage contact between students and faculty are elements of this approach.

These and other efforts work to foster resilience among students and shift behavioral norms to lower overall risk of suicide.[11]

Increasing help-seeking behaviors among students at greatest risk is another essential component of this broad public health approach and can help save lives. IHE counseling centers reduce the suicide rate for their clients to one-sixth of what otherwise would be expected.[12] Having high-profile campus members model the desired behavior is a particularly effective way of reducing the stigma of seeking help. If a senior administrator or faculty member is willing to report a successful personal experience with counseling, it can have a significant impact on a campus that values academic achievement. At Cornell University, President Skorton talked about his own experience of benefiting from counseling and exhorted students, "If you learn anything at Cornell, learn to ask for help. It is a sign of wisdom and strength."

Despite efforts that encourage help seeking, some students in need of care will not pursue services. Therefore it is important to educate all members of the community about how to identify struggling students and connect them with resources. At Cornell, we have developed a program called "Notice and Respond" that prepares faculty, staff, teaching assistants, and students to recognize and respond effectively to students in distress. These facilitated discussions use dramatized video vignettes to portray how bystanders overcome barriers and reach out to a student in need. The sessions have proven effective in conveying the importance of the role of each member of the community in supporting students.

A key to the success of "Notice and Respond" has been gaining access to target populations. The sessions, which last from fifty to ninety minutes, are presented at monthly faculty and staff department meetings, and the student version, called Friend2Friend, is presented in academic classes to all first-year students in one of the university's largest colleges.

Cornell also reaches some students who might be hesitant to access traditional counseling services through a successful program called "Let's Talk," staffed by psychologists and social workers. This program provides easy access to informal, confidential consultations at various walk-in sites across campus. We developed another program called "Community Consultation and Intervention" that dedicates two mental health professionals who provide consultation to key campus partners such as academic advisers, faculty, and residence life staff. They also provide direction around difficult student situations, training, advocacy, and case-management services, as well as crisis intervention.

One inherent challenge in this broad public health approach is that it often will, if successful, lead to more students seeking professional mental health care. This raises an important question for all colleges and universities about how much mental health care they can provide and to what level of staffing they should aspire. The International Association of Counseling Services (IACS), an accrediting body for many college and university counseling services, suggests having one counselor for every one thousand to fifteen hundred students.[13] This ratio provides an important touchstone but does not consider a number of relevant variables, such as whether the institution is located in a rural or urban environment. Urban environments generally have more referral options, and students may be more likely to seek out those resources on their own. Urban areas also provide more options for off-campus psychiatric services, an important factor to consider when deciding whether to make those services available on campus. Other variables include the size of the institution and its public or private status. Small private colleges tend to hold different expectations among students, alumni, parents, faculty, and staff. A ratio of one counselor for every five hundred to seven hundred students may be appropriate, whereas a larger state institution may be able to meet the demand with one counselor for every two thousand or twenty-five hundred students. Benchmarking data at comparable institutions is helpful in determining the best counselor-to-student ratio.

Another key question related to counseling services is how those services are provided. In the past decade, Cornell University has offered brief assessments over the phone, thus allowing therapists to make determinations about students most in need of care. We also expanded hours, offering phone and walk-in assessment and consultation in the evenings and on weekends. We treat the student's physical and mental health in an integrated manner, which opens the door for primary care settings to facilitate access to counseling services for ambivalent students. We screen for depression, alcohol abuse, and anxiety in primary care visits and encourage collaboration among treatment providers through interdisciplinary teams.

Another component of providing care to a college or university community is to develop effective coordinated responses when a crisis does occur on campus. This often includes having health and counseling staff available 24-7 to respond by phone and maintaining a strong working relationship with emergency departments and mental health units at local hospitals. Local suicide hotlines can also augment the campus network of support, as can the availability of experienced student affairs staff to serve as crisis managers when there is a student crisis, death, or suicide. These individuals can coordinate travel arrangements with families and manage other logistical issues related to the crisis. Another critical step is to have a community support team made up of student and academic support staff, religious life staff, and mental health professionals, to facilitate meetings with affected individuals and communities. The goals of these meetings are to share information, assist with the grieving process, and offer support resources. Various authors have outlined more extensively how these meetings can be structured and managed.[14]

A final component of a comprehensive public health approach is to review the relative safety of the physical environment and restrict access to lethal approaches that students could take. The Harvard School of Public Health, on its "Means Matters" website, states that "a number of studies have indicated that when lethal means are made less available or less deadly, suicide rates by that method decline, and frequently suicide rates overall decline. This has been demonstrated in a number of areas: bridge barriers, detoxification of domestic gas, pesticides, medication packaging, and others." They go on to state that "while some suicides are deliberative and involve careful planning, many appear to have an impulsive component and occur during a short-term crisis," underscoring the importance of means restriction. On most campuses, this means prohibiting firearms or offering lockers for gun owners to store firearms; closely tracking, monitoring, and controlling access to toxic substances found in laboratories, pharmacies, and other departments; and restricting access to high places (such as rooftops, windows, bridges, and balconies).[15]

This broad public health approach with a focus on the physical environment has also led some faculty and student support staff to think about how the physical environment can go beyond basic restriction from harm to being a part of expanding overall wellness. On multiple campuses, students and other community members are now encouraged to spend more time in nature. The idea that spending time in nature is good for us psychologically, emotionally, and spiritually is a long-standing belief across count-less cultures. The rest of this book will review the literature on the positive impacts of time spent in nature. We will also discuss ways to build programs that facilitate time in nature among the students on your campus.

2

The Proven Benefits of Spending Time in Nature

Belief in the benefits of spending time in nature has precedents that stretch back thousands of years. In *On the Parts of Animals*, Aristotle said, "For in all natural things there is something marvellous."[1] The transcendentalist writer Ralph Waldo Emerson mused in his essay "Nature" that "the lover of nature is he whose inward and outward senses are still truly adjusted to each other; who has retained the spirit of infancy even into the era of manhood."[2] The great naturalist John Muir wrote in his journals, "Nature's peace will flow into you as sunshine flows into trees. The winds will blow their own freshness into you, and the storms their energy, while cares will drop off like autumn leaves."[3] This sense was also expressed by the great environmental writer Rachel Carson, who wrote in *Silent Spring*, "There is something infinitely healing in the repeated refrains of nature—the assurance that dawn comes after night, and spring after winter."[4]

Impact of Time in Nature on Reducing Stress and Increasing Concentration

In recent decades, an impressive number of studies have been undertaken to both increase our understanding and provide scientific validation of the myriad ways in which spending time in nature contributes to our well-being. Two benefits of particular interest to college-aged students are an increased ability to concentrate and a reduction in stress levels in response to time spent in green spaces. In the 1990s Stephen and Rachel Kaplan developed a theoretical explanation for the relationship between loss of concentration and stress called attention restoration theory. The theory postulates that prolonged use of directed (voluntary) attention, as demanded by most occupations and academic study, causes us to experience mental fatigue and associated irritability and stress. Spending even a brief period in the natural world promotes a sense of involuntary fascination that allows the brain's directed attention to rest and recover from the rigors of problem solving.[5] The result, according to the Kaplans, is a more relaxed state and an increased ability to attend to tasks.

In 2003, Terry Hartig and colleagues published results of a study that examined the Kaplans' attention restoration theory in 112 young adults. They divided subjects into equal-sized cohorts and subjected them to either an environmental treatment (viewing trees out a window, followed by a walk through a nature reserve) or an urban treatment (sitting in a windowless room followed by a walk through an urban area). Not only did members of the environmental group experience a significant reduction in blood pressure thirty minutes into the walk relative to the urban group, but they also displayed improved performance on a postwalk concentration test.[6]

The attention restoration theory has particular relevance in our contemporary social media–saturated culture. Exploring the connection between time in nature and brain functioning more deeply, a research group exposed fifty-six adults to a four-day nature immersion during which participants had no access to electronic technology. They found that individuals displayed a 50 percent improvement in creative problem-solving tasks relative to before the nature experience. They speculated that the result is attributable to both the natural stimuli of the outdoor environment along with an absence of attention-demanding technology.[7]

In contrast to attention restoration, the stress-reduction theory of Roger Ulrich and colleagues focuses even more specifically on how we respond to external stressors, and posits that our responses occur through changes in our physiology.[8] According to this theory, time spent in natural settings, or even viewing natural scenes out a window or on a screen, can result in positive changes in physiological activity levels and lead to a more positively toned emotional state.

A distinctly Japanese approach to the stress-reduction theory is called forest bathing, or *shinrin-yoku* in Japanese, a mindfulness-based relaxation approach first popularized in the 1990s. In a study of forest bathing that 280 Japanese college-aged students participated in, subjects walked mindfully through one of twenty-four forested areas or through an urban site for an equal length of time. In post-test evaluations, salivary cortisol concentrations (long used as a measure of stress levels in humans), blood pressure, pulse rate, and heart rate were lower in the forest bathers than the city walkers,[9] meaning that stress levels were significantly reduced. A similar study by Japanese researchers found that fifteen-minute walks taken by young men through either an urban park or city streets resulted in the park strollers having higher levels of para-sympathetic nervous activity (involved with slower heart rates and relaxing sphincter muscles) and lower levels of sympathetic nervous activity (responsible for stimulating activities associated with the fight-or-flight response) than those who walked along city streets.[10]

FIGURE 2-1
Forest bathing
(Courtesy of Lindsay France, Cornell University Photography)

Stress levels in post-secondary students can either be incidental (prior to a big exam or just after an interpersonal conflict, for example) or chronic (felt every day, especially on waking). Chronic stress can lead to serious, long-term psychological conditions, including rumination (the "maladaptive pattern of self-referential thought that is associated with heightened risk of depression and other mental illnesses"),[11] depression, and chronic fatigue syndrome.[12] For those students chronically plagued by high stress levels, it can be vitally important to devise a path toward resiliency, which is the ability to regain health and a calm or positive outlook following sickness, depression misfortune, or disappointment. Resiliency is often associated with the maintenance of a stable equilibrium, even when the underlying psychological condition persists.[13]

Gregory Bratman and colleagues focused on the impact of time in nature on reducing rumination patterns. They asked thirty-eight healthy individuals to take a ninety-minute walk through a natural area on a college campus or through a heavily urbanized environment. The results were dramatic: those who walked in natural settings experienced reduced levels of rumination and lower activation of the subgenual prefrontal cortex (sgPFC), a portion of the brain linked to rumination in both healthy and depressed individuals.[14] These researchers did not, however, conduct a longitudinal study to determine longer-term effects on participants' sgPFC levels.

In a study that examined the impact of adventure experiences (AEs) on building resiliency, eighty-five college students enrolled in either a traditional classroom-based course or an adventure-based expedition, involving such activities as rock climbing, winter camping, mountain climbing, and wilderness survival, both of which lasted three weeks. Students in both groups completed a survey reflecting their self-assessment of resiliency just before and immediately after their respective experience ended. The AE participants reported significantly increased senses of overall resiliency, while the classroom participants did not. In addition, a select group of AE participants who were contacted two to three years after the test were able to recount specific memories that contributed to their bolstered and ongoing sense of resiliency.[15]

As explained in chapter 1, college and university students are increasingly experiencing serious mental health concerns, especially stress, anxiety, and depression. Contact with the natural environment can contribute substantially to healing and the development of resilience.[16] In a study of twenty individuals diagnosed with major depressive disorder, positive affect and mood improved to a much greater extent after a nature walk than after an urban walk. Nature walkers also improved their working memory capacity.[17]

A research project in Australia looked at a small cohort of women between the ages of seventeen and twenty-one, all of whom had been suffering from a range of physical and substance abuse problems and severe difficulties with families or other associates. Of the seven women who enrolled in the six-week program, five agreed to undertake a grueling twelve-day wilderness adventure experience. Though physically and psychologically difficult for the participants, all five women reported after they completed the trek that they improved their self-management of physical and mental health issues; reduced their dependence on drugs and alcohol; and improved capacities to connect socially.[18]

Green Spaces and College Campuses

Approaches to improving mood and cognition that depend on intensive, multiday experiences in challenging natural environments would be difficult to make accessible to a broad range of college and university students. Yet many college and university campuses abound with natural, pastoral, or horticultural sites that students can access, even with busy academic schedules.

Returning to the Kaplans' attention restoration theory, there are four qualities that are essential for a site to qualify as restorative:[19]

- Being away from the norm: being physically separate from where one normally is, with a distinct feel to the setting.
- Having a sense of extent: being large enough to allow one to move around and see the area as a connected whole.
- Providing a sense of compatibility: based on the individual's past experience, it should be familiar enough to provide a sense of comfort, yet still retain a quality of discovery.
- Being rooted in fascination: fascination, in the Kaplans' sense, is similar to what the philosopher William James called "involuntary

attention." Natural settings lend themselves to a sense of fascination, whether one is walking along a wooded pathway, sitting by
a stream, or trying to identify spring-migrating birds. In any of
these settings one's fascination with the natural surroundings su-
persedes one's directed attention, allowing that function to rest.

These qualities can be found on college campuses in small
wooded areas, on grassy quadrangles, or even along tree-lined sidewalks; such spaces do not need to resemble the forest primeval to
be beneficial to students. In a study conducted at a university in
Texas researchers found that those students who self-identified as
"high users" of campus green settings rated their overall quality of
life higher when compared to students who used such spaces less
frequently.[20] In another research project, students at a British university responded to a survey on campus green spaces by indicating
that they strongly preferred managed green spaces, such as lawns
and athletic fields, over more naturalistic areas. Most students made
the most use of green spaces adjacent to their classrooms, dorms,
or labs, using them primarily for socializing and decompressing.[21]

This finding is consistent with Ulrich's evolutionary theory that
humans have a predisposition toward open, savanna-like conditions (think, expansive lawn) and are inherently less comfortable
in spatially restricted settings that may contain hidden dangers
and limit opportunities for escape.[22] Based on this, designers of
academic campuses might best serve their constituencies by pro-
posing multiple open green spaces within close walking distance
from popular gathering sites, rather than leaving large expanses of
woodlands or thickets untouched.

It may not even be necessary for students to be *out* in nature to
derive benefits from campus green spaces. A group of seventy-two
undergraduates residing in dormitories at a midwestern university
had views from their dorm room windows that were categorized

FIGURE 2-2
A college green at Swarthmore College
(Courtesy of The Scott Arboretum)

as either all natural (trees, grass, shrubs, water); mostly natural (some trees and turf, along with paths, roads, etc.); mostly built (few trees, mostly parking lots and buildings); and entirely built (view blocked by other buildings). Researchers reported that those students in the first two categories performed significantly better on a series of directed attention tests than those who were deprived of natural views.[23]

For campuses in northern climates the question arises of whether nature is as restorative in winter months—when trees are bare, flowers are absent, and lawns are brown or snow covered—as it is during the growing season. In a study conducted at a northern US university, students were instructed to imagine themselves to be mentally fatigued, and then spent time viewing four settings: (1) no views of nature; (2) views through windows of late fall with leafless trees and some built structures; (3) views of wall-sized murals of fields or fully leafed trees; and (4) views of wall-sized murals of a seacoast or waterfall. Unsurprisingly, in evaluating the restorative properties of each of the views, the students ranked the windowless setting as the lowest. But both settings with the wall-sized murals were rated as *more* restorative than the window view of bare trees. Thus, even viewing pictures of lush nature can help restore directed attention in college-aged populations.[24] We may speculate, however, that actually spending time outside in nature is more beneficial than looking at nature images or staring at a framed window view.

Increasingly, colleges and universities house some form of botanical garden, arboretum, or display gardens on their grounds. Some, like Swarthmore College in Swarthmore, Pennsylvania, consider their entire campus a public garden. Swarthmore's is named the Scott Arboretum. Others, like the Arnold Arboretum of Harvard University or the Morris Arboretum of the University of Pennsylvania, are quite extensive but physically distant from their main campuses.

A study that examined the potential role of botanic gardens on reducing stress in visitors to three Florida-based gardens found that perceived tension levels decreased dramatically as a result of the visit, and most significantly for those with the highest depression index scores.[25] Another research project used means-end analysis to examine the attributes, consequences, and values that visitors apply to a university-based botanic garden. While over half of respondents indicated that they used their visits for relaxation and stress relief, it was the strongest concept link for student respondents, who used stress relief and relaxation to attain an improved quality of life.[26] Applying this finding to higher education institutions, the presence of a botanic garden or arboretum on campus could serve as a pressure relief valve for highly stressed students. This concept will be further explored in chapter 3.

Finally, while our primary focus is on the effects of time spent in nature, a growing body of evidence also supports the stress relief that results from engaging in gardening. A Dutch study subjected participants to stress-inducing activities, then engaged individuals in either light garden work in their allotments or time spent reading. Gardening and reading each led to lower salivary cortisol levels during the recovery period, but decreases were significantly stronger in the gardening group. Positive mood was fully restored after gardening but further deteriorated after reading.[27] These findings corroborate earlier studies on the positive impact of gardening on mental health.[28]

How the Body Reacts to Time Spent in Nature

A significant US health crisis that shows no signs of abating is obesity in children and teens. Obesity, defined as having a gross excess of body fat, today affects nearly 20 percent of all children and adolescents between the ages of five and nineteen.[29] While inappropriate diet is certainly a causal factor, so are inadequate levels of exercise. A significant factor contributing to sedentary lifestyles is screen time. Young people have dramatically increased the number of hours they spend on all types of media each day, with a current average of 7 and a half hours per day, seven days per week.[30]

Concurrently, the involvement of young people with any type of exercise, and particularly exercise outdoors in nature, has fallen precipitously. The 2017 participation report of the Physical Activity Council found that 17.9 percent of six- to twelve-year-olds, and 18.4 percent of thirteen- to seventeen-year-olds were essentially inactive.[31] And a 2013 National Outdoor Recreation Report found that just over half of adolescent girls participated in outdoor recreation of any kind, the lowest rate recorded since that report began in 2006.[32] As described previously, *any* time spent in nature is beneficial, but when young people couple being outside with exercising, taking even a short walk, it can contribute to the attainment of a healthy lifestyle and reduce the likelihood of obesity.

The previous discussion of attention restoration theory and stress-reduction theory focused primarily on the *psychological* effect of time spent in nature. Building on this, an exciting recent research thrust has been an examination of the physiological and biological mechanisms underlying such benefits.

Some compounds naturally found in plants may have been directly affecting how our bodies function for thousands of years, without our being consciously aware of them. Phytoncides are volatile organic compounds given off by many plants, including onion, garlic, tea tree, oak, cedar, locust, and pine. When these molecules are taken in through nasal passages, they have been shown to both reduce blood pressure by reducing sympathetic nerve activity and boost immune functioning by enhancing human natural killer (NK) cell activity.[33]

Even soil-borne compounds could be impacting human well-being. *Mycobacterium vaccae* are nonpathogenic bacterial compounds commonly found in soils. When introduced to mice, they stimulated a newly discovered group of neurons, which in turn increased levels of serotonin (associated with feelings of well-being and happiness) and decreased levels of anxiety.[34] A second research group, which separated mice between those that were fed mycobacterium and a control group that was not, found that the former group navigated a maze twice as fast and with less demonstrated anxiety behavior than the control mice.[35]

Ming Kuo of the University of Illinois at Urbana-Champaign has proposed a central pathway for the ways in which contact with nature promotes human health. In multiple ways, she posits, the nature experience positively impacts immune system activity.[36] As previously described, one mechanism for this is an increase in NK cells. These cells are an innate component of the immune system, providing rapid responses to viral-infected cells. In two additional Japanese forest-bathing experiments, a three-day trip to a forested setting resulted in increased NK cell activity and the expression of anticancer proteins in both males[37] and females, and for the female subjects the effects lasted at least seven days after the trip.[38]

In addition to fighting viral and other infections, an enhanced immune system plays important health-promoting roles in reducing the likelihood of autoimmune disorders, facilitating healthy pregnancies, healing wounds, and destroying tumor cells.[39] In addition, time spent in nature results in reduced levels of inflammatory cytokines and blood glucose levels. Cytokines are released by the immune system in response to a threat or scare, and have been implicated with diabetes, cardiovascular disease, and depression. Elevated blood glucose levels, in turn, have been associated with blindness, nerve damage, and kidney failure.[40]

Kuo does not argue that an enhanced immune system is the only mechanism by which contact with nature promotes health. She acknowledges that attention restoration, improved sleep patterns, deep relaxation, and improved social ties may each play an additional role. But her detailed analysis not only provides robust evidence for the mechanisms by which time spent in nature has positive and measurable health benefits, but also demonstrates that the cumulative effect of these benefits could be impacting the body's functions in ways that had not previously been imagined.[41]

What Is the Correct Dose of Time in Nature?

Several of the previously cited studies contrasted the effects of time spent in natural settings with equal durations spent in urban sites. Some researchers have raised questions about the most effective time doses in nature. Jo Barton and Jules Pretty examined ten prior studies that had been conducted at the University of Exeter in England to determine the best dose of green exercise for affecting both mood and self-esteem. They concluded that both of these measures of well-being showed the greatest changes after only five minutes of green exercise. After that, improvements continued for up to one hour, but at diminished rates. They also found that self-esteem improvements actually declined with growing intensity of activity, demonstrating that lighter activity (walking, strolling) may provide greater benefits than intensive green exercise.[42]

In a related experiment, researchers at the University of Michigan asked forty-four participants to immerse themselves in nature at least 2.5 times per week for eight weeks. Subjects were free to have each experience last from ten minutes up to an hour. Both before and immediately after each green exercise event, participants answered questions about their mental well-being and their ability to concentrate was assessed. These were then correlated to the subjects' salivary cortisol levels, as an indicator of stress levels. After just ten minutes in nature, stress indexes went down, and participants reported improvements in their focus, mood, and energy levels. While all of these indexes continued to improve after greater time durations, it was again at a reduced rate of increase.[43]

Spending time in nature has gone from an activity assumed to be good for us to one with multiple identified biopsychosocial benefits, regardless of one's mental or physical health. We also now know that benefits can be detected in as little as five to ten minutes, but that they continue to accrue beyond that, albeit at lower rates. Even what constitutes a "nature experience" must be determined subjectively, as shown by English college students who preferred more managed green spaces to more naturalistic ones. Students can take advantage of multiple, easily accessible green oases scattered across a campus to reduce their stress, rumination, and depression levels, improve memory and cognition, and even reduce the likelihood of illness. The challenge, then, is finding ways to convince students to spend that time outdoors.

3

Developing a Nature Rx Program on a College Campus

Background

When one pictures a modern college or university campus, one typically imagines the significant events occurring inside buildings—the classrooms, research labs, and residence halls. In this chapter, we put forth a radically different notion: that many of the rich experiences at an institute of higher learning can take place outside those ivy-covered walls, on the lawns and greens and in the gardens and woodlands that allow for a reconnection with the natural world.

For some students, regular communing with nature may be as ingrained as brushing their teeth. For others, particularly individuals coming from urban backgrounds, structures or incentives need to be provided to encourage them to venture into the great outdoors.

Model Programs

College and university administrators can learn from the number of community-based programs that have been initiated over the past few years that encourage young people in different age groups to actively engage with parks and green spaces. The best known of these was started under the title DC Park Rx, a partnership between the Washington, DC, chapter of the American Academy of Pediatrics and the National Park Service. DC pediatricians felt that it would be relatively simple for participating doctors to add a park prescription to the electronic health record of patients. Starting in 2010, trained volunteers working for the program identified and rated 342 DC-area parks on the bases of cleanliness, accessibility, level of activity, amenities, and safety. In the pilot program, health professionals at one Unity Health Care site were trained in how to access the DC Park Rx database and to use it to match individual patient's interests and home location to the park that would best serve them.

Parents of participating patients reported on the program's effectiveness: a significantly increased number of these parents believed that physical activity positively affected the health of their child; and young people's average weekly physical activity increased by 15 percent, as did average number of days spent in parks.[1]

Based on the success of the pilot, the program has been rebranded as Park Rx America, whose mission is to "decrease the burden of chronic disease, increase health and happiness, and foster environmental stewardship, by virtue of prescribing Nature during the routine delivery of healthcare."[2] With nearly twenty health- and outdoor-based partner organizations, the program has enrolled fifty physicians from clinics in DC, Maryland, Virginia, Washington, and Alaska. As of this writing, they have collectively written over three thousand nature prescriptions.

In Columbus, Ohio, a progressive cardiologist named David Sabgir found himself frustrated that speaking to clients in his office was having little effect on getting them to change their behavior. So on a Saturday morning in the spring of 2005, he invited patients to

FIGURE 3-1
The founder of Walk with a Doc, David Sabgir, leading an event at Highbanks Metro Park
(Courtesy of Walk with a Doc)

join him on a walk through a park. To his surprise, over one hundred people showed up, energized and ready to move.

From this rudimentary beginning, the Walk with a Doc movement has grown as a grassroots effort, with a model based on sustainability and simplicity. Since hiring an executive director to steer growth in 2009, the organization now has over three hundred chapters worldwide. For each event at every chapter, the sponsoring physician starts with a brief presentation on a health topic and then leads participants on a walk at their own pace.

Based on the Walk with a Doc model, in 2011 the Frederick County, Maryland, Department of Parks and Recreation launched

FIGURE 3-2
Children playing outdoors as part of an activity sponsored by LiveWell Greenville
(Courtesy of LiveWell Greenville)

its own Docs in the Parks program as a way to overcome major barriers to getting underserved families engaged with nature—including safety concerns, lack of familiarity with parks, and skepticism on the part of many pediatricians that their clients would have the time and motivation to participate in self-improvement programs. Working through a coalition of not-for-profits, the initiative regularly sponsors events in parks to further its mission to "promote the health of children by connecting families with local healthy foods and increasing opportunities for active outdoor play in nature."[3]

LiveWell Greenville involves a large human services network focused on reducing the high levels of obesity in Greenville County, South Carolina, where 66 percent of adults and 41 percent of young people are overweight or obese. Hosted by the YMCA of Greenville, LiveWell has become the primary vehicle through which partner organizations can successfully promote healthy eating and active living. Using community based participatory research principles, the coalition welcomes the input of the community in developing, implementing, and evaluating initiatives. In an effort to increase physical activity in or near school settings, the partners worked to fund the Bike Trailer initiative through which bikes are dropped off at schools to be utilized in physical education classes in fourth and fifth grades. And to create a stronger link with the medical community, the Physicians as Liaisons in Schools (PALS) initiative encourages active participation of a doctor on each school wellness team.[4]

Programs similar to those just described have been created in San Francisco, San Diego, and Portland, Oregon. Common to each initiative is that they engage the medical community in prescribing time in nature; they are built on partnerships or coalitions of like-minded agencies and organizations; and they recognize the importance of having young people spend time in nature, both actively in recreation or passively enjoying nature's beauty.

Bringing Nature Rx to College Students

Just as municipal leaders, health professionals, and community organizers care about the welfare of residents and patients, college and university administrators are constantly searching for ways to ensure the well-being of the students with whom they have been entrusted. But how can such municipal models be transferred to a college or university campus? Campus landscapes vary widely, from bucolic sites with wide lawns and sylvan oases, to urban settings with restricted grounds and few natural areas. Also, while municipalities like Columbus and Baltimore can form partnerships with multiple agencies and organizations to carry out their work, institutions of higher learning typically depend on their internal resources to address student needs.

In this and the following chapters, we will use the generic term "Nature Rx" to refer to all college- or university-based programs whose goals are to encourage students to spend more time in nature to contribute to their well-being and their appreciation of the natural world. While recognizing that each school's program has unique features, what follows is a series of general steps that can be taken to develop and sustain a Nature Rx program on a college or university campus.

Step 1: Organize a Committed Group

Every campus has individuals who are advocates for the health and welfare of the student body. Most faculty members fall into this category, as do the medical and psychological professionals at the campus health center, the student services staff, and student members of clubs that focus on mental health. If the school has a botanic garden or arboretum, a representative from this unit should also be involved. Add to this mix campus community members who are passionate about environmental protection and you have the nucleus of a Nature Rx steering committee.

Ideally, this group would comprise a broad representation of faculty, staff, and both undergraduate and graduate students, with a total number of no more than twelve. At an initial meeting of the group, one individual should be appointed chair and another as recorder of meeting minutes. To maintain energy and focus, it is recommended that members have term limits, and that the chairmanship rotate every two to three years. Other logistical details—where and how often to meet, terms of office, posting of meeting notices and minutes—can also be addressed at this initial get-together. More critical, however, is deciding on the mission and goals of the committee. Once the mission has been discussed and agreed to, a series of goals can be articulated for the first year, or the first two to three years. These will serve as benchmarks against which to gauge the progress the committee is making in support of the mission.

Step 2: Secure the Support of the Administration

To ensure that the efforts of the Nature Rx steering committee reach the entire campus, it's critical for the school administration to be fully supportive of the group's mission. Even if there is no commitment of campus funds, having administrators behind the initiative will open doors to campus units that might otherwise be resistant. Given the many conflicting demands on their time and attention, it is unlikely that the top-level administrators— typically the president and provost—will be reachable. But the next tier down, such as the vice president for student affairs or dean of students, should be asked by the steering committee chair to officially endorse the mission and goals of the Nature Rx group. To attract such individuals to the cause, the best strategy might be to emphasize the research that has confirmed the psychological and physiological benefits of time in nature (see chapter 2).

An officer of the school who has expressed his or her support for the Nature Rx mission should be considered an ally and advocate. He or she should be invited to participate in Nature Rx–sponsored activities, such as nature walks. This individual should also be included in meetings at which major strategic approaches are to be discussed, especially if they may impact the senior administration.

Step 3: Inventory Green Spaces on Campus

While campuses differ greatly in their overall amount of green space, virtually all colleges and universities have some verdant spots to which students can escape. A valuable early project for the Nature Rx team to take on would be the development of an inventory of all natural, naturalistic, or horticultural spaces on campus. If the school employs an in-house landscape architect, this effort would be greatly facilitated by engaging him or her.

For each site to be included in the inventory, the following criteria should be analyzed:

- Nature of the site: woodland, lawn, garden, creek, gorge, etc.
- Special qualities: shade, water feature, low noise level, benches, etc.
- Overall size in square feet or square meters
- Accessibility: whether it is accessible and traversable to individuals with limited or no mobility
- Distance from central location (such as the administration building or residence hall)

Nature Rx groups on urban campuses may be surprised by the number of sites they are able to identify. The size of such sites is a much less important factor than their accessibility and the features that they offer. If, however, the results of the inventory on a particular campus reveal a paucity of available green sites, this data may serve to drive the school to create additional oases. Perhaps an underutilized parking area can be converted to a meadow, or the site where a no longer functional building is to be removed can become a garden. The completed inventory can also serve as the basis of a Nature Rx website or app, described later in this section.

Step 4: Engage the Students

There are a number of ways in which students could get engaged in the Nature Rx initiative. The first of these is to develop a student advisory group, made up of representatives from student clubs that have an outdoor or environmental focus. Examples of these representative associations might be a hiking club, a sustainability corps, a Green Party chapter, or a wilderness adventure group. The primary role of this advisory group would be to develop programming and marketing ideas and funnel them back to the steering committee. As such, communication is best facilitated if one of the members of the advisory group is also a member of the steering committee. Since all students are busy, the number of meetings per semester might be limited to two.

An alternative to the student advisory group would be a student-led Nature Rx club. (The actual name of the group is unimportant, and students may prefer one with more immediate appeal). This club could sponsor such things as weekly nature walks, natural area cleanups or invasive plant removals, geocaching contests, trips to nearby or regional natural wonders, or outdoor recreation events, such as Frisbee tosses. The student club will need a faculty adviser, both to serve as a liaison to the Nature Rx steering committee and to help the club through challenging periods, such as when the group's leadership changes or during stressful exam periods. Clubs often follow a pattern of starting with great enthusiasm, and then declining in activities and participation as the semester becomes more demanding. The faculty adviser can be alert to this issue and explore ways of maintaining engagement.

FIGURE 3-3
Robert Zarr and Don Rakow leading a Nature Rx walk
(Photo by the authors)

Students know how best to advertise to fellow students, whether through social media, chalking on sidewalks, or placing posters in strategic spots (dormitory hallways, cafeterias, restrooms, etc.). A faculty member of the steering committee could offer a particularly ambitious and media-savvy student independent study credit to market the Nature Rx initiative throughout the semester. The student could then be evaluated on such metrics as the number of promotions they develop, the innovativeness of their approach, or the number of students attracted to particular activities.

Yet another approach is to engage students directly in featured activities. This is at the heart of the University of California–Davis Learning by Leading initiative described further in chapter 4. Students who are directly involved in activities such as growing organic vegetable gardens, clearing invasives out of campus woodlands, or monitoring streamside populations of amphibians are more likely to become passionate about the environment and their role in protecting it. As they share their newly gained knowledge with fellow undergraduates or graduate fellows, they will develop leadership skills that can carry into their poststudent lives.

Step 5: Partner with Campus Health Services

Nearly every member of the student body winds up at the campus health facility sometime during the school year. Based on the park prescription model described earlier, health professionals at the clinic can be encouraged to initiate a nature prescription program for students who they determine would benefit from extra time in nature. Given the many verified benefits (see chapter 2), students given nature prescriptions might include those suffering from stress or depression, sleep deprivation, physical cutting, obesity or inactivity, or social isolation.

At this time, it is unclear whether the prescription is more effective in paper form or as part of the student's electronic health record. For either approach, the nature prescription should offer options of where to spend time in nature on campus, and recommend the frequency with which he or she should venture out into green spaces. Just the engagement of physicians and clinicians in recognizing the benefits of time spent in nature can impact the thinking and outlook of students and the faculty who advise them.

Often the campus health center will employ a communications coordinator, and this person can be extremely helpful in publicizing upcoming events or initiatives, usually at no cost to the steering committee.

Step 6: Develop an App or Website

Once the natural areas inventory described in step 3 has been completed, it can serve as the basis for an app or responsive website dedicated to the Nature Rx program. Features that might be included are descriptions and images of each of the natural or landscaped areas on campus, including the level of difficulty of traversing the area; maps showing how to reach each of these sites (if the app or website is GPS-based, it can also display how to reach the nearest green space); seasons in which particular spaces are at their best; suggested activities with which to become involved outdoors; and links to scientific studies verifying the benefits of spending time in nature, as well as to student clubs that have an outdoor or environmental focus.

The tricky thing about an app or website is that you want students to use it to learn and get excited about campus green spaces, but you don't want them depending on it while they are actually out in nature. One way to achieve this is to state on the site, "While out in nature, put down your phone or iPad and use your senses to see, hear, smell, and fully experience what is around you." The app or website can also provide links to a Facebook, Instagram, Twitter, or other social media site on which students can post their comments or photos, and upcoming events could be promoted.

Step 7: Impact the Academic Program

There are two primary approaches when trying to make changes to a school's academic program: curriculum-based or site-based. In the first approach, new classes are developed that focus on activities out in nature and the benefits to be derived from them. Both the University of Minnesota's Nature Heals course and UC Davis's Nature Rx course are examples of this; they are described in detail in chapter 4.

If a college or university instructor is considering the creation of such a course, it is critical to address what one is trying to achieve with the curriculum:

- Is it simply to expose students to various natural and landscaped sites on campus with which they might not yet be familiar? This may appeal to first-year students in particular.
- Is it to blend time spent in green spaces with the arts and humanities, such as assigning readings from authors like Thoreau or Emerson, requiring students to write journal entries or poems, or holding dance or music performances in the woods?
- Is it to overtly relate time in nature to various psychological, physiological, or attitudinal benefits? Activities could then include mindfulness meditation, yoga, or forest bathing, and readings could include scientific papers in which such benefits have been rigorously studied.
- Finally, is it to increase environmental appreciation among students? In that case, field trips could include visits to both healthy ecosystems as well as degraded ones for comparison, and readings could focus on ecopsychology, field ecology, or ecological restoration.

Site-based changes to an academic program simply involve getting instructors to take their classes outside—regardless of the discipline—at least once per semester. It may seem crazy to suggest that a French class or a nuclear physics course meet out of doors. But it is likely to be a memorable experience for the students involved, which could result in their retaining more of the material the instructor covers. The Nature Rx steering committee might even promote a "Take Your Class Outside" month, such as October in the north when autumn beauty is at its peak.

A variation on the site-based approach is for an existing course to hold some classes in natural or landscaped sites to take advantage of the features that can meld the theoretical with the practical realm. For example, a structural engineering class might examine how a bridge over a campus creek was constructed, or a freehand drawing group might sketch tree structure in winter.

Step 8: Develop an Approach to Evaluation

Evaluation is often the step that's underdeveloped, ignored, or tackled only after the activity has been completed. An effective evaluation effort should combine front-end, formative, and summative elements in an integrated manner. Using as an example a new Nature Rx class, the front-end component would examine existing models, consider the potential audience members and their needs, and develop both a plan for the class and a rationale for why it is needed.

As the course is being offered, both anecdotal and formalized reactions from the students will allow the instructors to make midcourse corrections: perhaps the meeting room isn't conducive to the types of discussions that are expected, or transportation to the outdoor sites is inadequate. When rapid corrections can be made during the semester, it can greatly impact students' impressions of the class.

Finally, a summative evaluation asks the participants—in this case the students—to evaluate their overall experience: Did the course meet the stated learning objectives? Did it allow for adequate discussion? Did it change the ways in which students think about or interact with the natural world?

Conscientiously conducted evaluations can be extremely valuable, not only internally to assess the value and impact of the effort, but as evidence to use with university administrators or potential funding sources. New courses are often initiated on a pilot basis, and a Nature Rx course that is positively evaluated by students has a better chance of being placed in the regular curriculum.

Step 9: Identify and Overcome the Challenges

Undergraduate students develop habits and preferences early in their college or university life. Between taking classes, studying, writing papers, engaging in sports, socializing, and partying, students may feel that they simply have no time left to commune with nature. Evidence shows, however, that as little as ten to fifteen minutes intentionally spent in nature can have a demonstrated effect on a young person's stress levels, mood, and ability to concentrate. Every student has at least that much discretionary time in a day, and even the most urban campus has green spaces to escape to for a few minutes.

Weather can be another challenge to address and overcome. In the north, it's the long, cold winters, and in the south and southwest one must deal with the oppressive heat of summer. But as Jeannie Larson of the Center for Spirituality and Healing at the University of Minnesota has said, to truly appreciate nature we must engage with it at all times, including when it's uncomfortable: "You need to push through it and get to the other side."[5]

To a degree, this is a matter of adjusting to the weather and wearing suitable clothing. Shorts and flip-flops are no more appropriate outdoors in a northern winter than sweatpants and hoodies are in a Georgia summer. In addition, the Nature Rx initiative should encourage activities that fit the season: when it's cold and snowy, sledding, cross-country skiing, or visits to an on-campus conservatory are all great activities to sponsor, and these can be replaced on hot summer days by creek walks, water balloon contests, and hikes in the shady woods.

A third internal challenge a Nature Rx enterprise may encounter is a lack of funding. As stated previously, the university may endorse the effort on some level but may provide no financial support for it. Fortunately, through the engagement of campus partners, a tremendous amount can be accomplished without a sizable budget. Individuals with expertise in marketing, website creation, poster design, outdoor education, curriculum development, and program evaluation may all be willing to support Nature Rx efforts, partly because they perceive the benefits of it to the student body, and partly because their salaries are already being covered through their regular duties.

Final Step: Model the Behavior

Hearkening back to the Frederick County Docs in the Park program, the presence of physicians in city parks there has encouraged area residents and their children to visit, be active in, and benefit from those recreational spaces. In a similar manner, the adults who students look to as role models—faculty members, residence hall advisers, health clinic professionals, and student services staff—can model healthy behavior by taking part in activities outdoors. The Nature Rx website or Facebook page could feature adults engaged in such easily achievable actions as a daily lunchtime walk or weekly mindfulness session in the woods.

By participating in these nature-oriented activities, adult role models achieve at least three things: they demonstrate that such activities are not difficult to engage in; they improve their own well-being, thus serving as examples of how nature can improve people's lives; and they serve as motivators to get more students involved in similar ways.

The end goal of any campus-based Nature Rx program is to contribute to the physical and psychological health of students. Getting a Nature Rx initiative off the ground may take some time, and having students change their habits is admittedly difficult, but given how valuable the outcome is, these are efforts that are well worth pursuing.

4

Nature Rx Programs on Four University Campuses

Background

The modern college or university campus can be thought of as a self-contained community comprising various academic buildings, libraries, residence halls, and student centers, and the grounds and infrastructure that surround these buildings. The term "campus," which is derived from the Latin word for "field," was first used in 1774 to describe a field adjacent to what is now Princeton University.[1] It wasn't until the twentieth century, however, that "campus" came to be associated with the entirety of the lands at institutions of higher learning.

The grounds of a college or university campus can have tremendous influence on young people's perceptions. If carefully laid out and spacious, a campus can influence an individual's decision to apply to study there. If well lit and open, it can add to students' sense of safety and serenity as they move about. And if it provides multiple spaces for gathering, it can inspire everything from outdoor classes to first dates.

Too often, however, higher education institutions have prioritized facilities over green spaces. As Janice C. Griffith wrote in an article on the preservation of open space on campuses, "In the face of skyrocketing enrollments and unprecedented technological developments that have dominated post-World War II campuses, inadequate attention has been paid to the importance of creating quality campus environments with adequate open space. As higher education communities seek to facilitate diversifying academic functions, more people, vehicular traffic, and ongoing technological advancements, they need to be reminded that open space must be treated as a scarce resource."[2]

In this chapter, we will focus on programs at four institutions, each of which uses the unique qualities of its grounds and location to promote engagement with nature and to increase pride in the campus.

UC Davis Learning by Leading

The UC Davis Arboretum was founded in 1936 by visionary faculty at UC Davis to support teaching and research at the University of California. In 2011, the UC Davis Arboretum and Public Garden (UCAPG) was formed, which recognized a merger between the Arboretum, the Putah Creek Riparian Reserve, and the Grounds and Landscape Services units. The Arboretum and Public Garden is responsible for the management of all outdoor spaces and non-research landscapes on the fifty-three hundred-acre campus, with the hundred-acre UC Davis Arboretum at its core.

Under the associate vice chancellor and director Kathleen Socolofsky, the UCAPG has evolved into one of the most innovative public gardens in North America. The UCAPG functions as an open door into campus, a physical pathway, and a thematic framework that unites landscapes and outreach centers along the two-mile length of the Arboretum and throughout the rest of campus. The UCAPG provides a variety of learning programs that allow visitors and students to connect the outdoors with the academic mission of the university. The UCAPG has an important mission: to demonstrate—through teaching landscapes, exhibits, and displays—some of the important ideas and complex issues UC Davis scholars are tackling. Sites and plant collections are used for teaching at UC Davis in dozens of STEM and agricultural education classes and beyond, and at other local K–12 schools and colleges, and they are used for research in a wide range of fields. The UCAPG provides a welcoming and engaging experience to visitors, is a vital experiential learning laboratory for undergraduate and graduate students, and serves as an innovative center for disseminating the work of campus researchers.

Shortly after arriving at UC Davis in 1998, Socolofsky led a cocreation process that resulted in the conception of the UC Davis GATEways Project to transform the outdoor landscapes of campus into both physical and programmatic gateways that share the riches of the university with the public. The resulting teaching landscapes, public art, pop-up exhibits, performances, and interactive programs by students link undergraduate learning with community engagement in the UCAPG and inspire students, faculty, staff, and visitors alike to spend time outdoors. The GATEways Project is now one of the foundational elements of a broader, campus-wide effort to create programs and landscapes that support a more holistic vision of sustainability that encompasses human health and well-being at its core. This new effort strives to positively impact the health and well-being of the UC Davis community and provides support, information, resources, and tools to help staff, faculty, and students to engage in healthy behaviors.

A core component of the GATEways Project is its Learning by Leading (LxL) internship program, based on the philosophy that students learn best when leading others. These leadership internships provide a training ground for students to learn real-world skills and lead efforts to create a healthier environment and a more sustainable world. The unique curriculum focuses on team-based, peer-led, experiential leadership lessons that prepare students to learn applied horticultural and ecological skills, lead with confidence through mentorships and hands-on teaching, and contribute to more attractive and sustainable campus spaces.

UCAPG staff works closely with over one hundred UC Davis undergraduate student interns per year in all areas of public garden operations, including nursery management, edible landscaping, sustainable horticulture, ecological restoration, creek stewardship, and environmental education and outreach. During their time at UC Davis, students have the opportunity to ascend the leadership ladder and tackle real-world issues. Continuing interns are encouraged to grow in their leadership and become student leaders or co-coordinators. By supervising less experienced interns, these co-coordinators gain valuable communication, interpersonal, supervisory, team-building, and time-management skills.

Nature-based interactions lie at the heart of all of these internships. Students are not sitting in classrooms being told about the importance of nature. They are outside installing native wetlands along the banks of the Arboretum Waterway for erosion control; converting turf medians into drought-tolerant gardens to save water and labor; pointing out caterpillars to the UCAPG's youngest visitors to hone their observational skills; or harvesting organic vegetables from plots they have planted and maintained to donate to the student food pantry on campus. Students gain horticulture skills through practical experience and leadership skills through direct application. One key value of these internships, as noted in a significant number of student testimonials, is how students are transported out of the classroom, dorm room, dining hall, or library and into the outdoors as active participants in their education, In the process, they experience the benefits of being immersed in nature.

The Environmental Education LxL interns develop programs for fellow UC students, children, families, and the general public to connect them with nature. Nearly all of these programs have a Nature Rx component to them, as the idea is to instill a love and appreciation of the outdoors. For instance, the Bugtopia series arms children with nets and encourages them to meet and examine the beneficial and pest insects they encounter in the gardens. LxL interns also develop programs with specific health and wellness themes, helping other students and the public learn to relax in nature. These programs include exercise, such as Yoga in the Arboretum, and nature experiences, such as Tea & Conversations on the Redwood Grove deck and Stargazing in the White Flower Garden.

The newest element of the GATEways Project is a Nature Rx freshman seminar. This weekly session introduces students to the living landscapes of UC Davis (including the Arboretum, Student Farm, Putah Creek Riparian Reserve, and other green spaces) and allows them to learn firsthand what makes each place unique. Goals of the seminar include exposing students to the gardens, green spaces, hidden nooks, and natural areas of UC Davis; introducing them to members of the faculty and staff who interact with nature on a regular basis through research or vocation; providing them with information about the therapeutic benefits associated with spending time in nature and the ways in which it can benefit one's health and sense of well-being; identifying the organizations that connect students to nature at UC Davis; and helping students reflect on the value of nature for their personal well-being.

Through walks, bike rides, and guided tours, students explore the natural components of UC Davis while simultaneously learning about activities and scientific research occurring all over campus. A sampling of the schedule offers a watercolor session along the banks of the Arboretum Waterway led by a landscape architecture professor; a yoga session and harvesting tour of the Student Farm; a tree walk to discover the favorite trees of the campus arborist; a chance to put on waders and identify fish with a professor of fish biology; and a tour of the botanical conservatory's greenhouses and exotic plants. In addition to exposing students to different experiences in and with nature, assigned reading and discussions focus on literature elucidating the health benefits associated with such activities. Introduced as a pilot in 2016, it has now

FIGURE 4-1
A UC Davis instructor with Learning by Leading students
(Courtesy of UC Davis Arboretum and Public Garden)

become a regular part of the UC Davis curriculum (see appendix A for the full course schedule).

Several students associated with Nature Rx have spoken of the program's great impact on them. One student, who we will identify by the initials SH, found the Nature Rx class to be destressing and a full immersion in nature. She also felt that it widened students' view of what they can do in nature, and that the class could potentially convert individuals who were skeptical about the value of time spent in nature. Through the Nature Rx class, SH learned about the student-run market garden, and signed on as an intern there.

Another student, MH, in the Waterway Stewardship Learning by Leading internship, captured the rewards of the program this way: "I think that I benefitted greatly from the tranquil moments of observation and contemplation in between the completion of tasks. . . . I feel that those almost meditative moments of work and observation also allowed me to be a more balanced and dynamic student both inside and outside of the classroom."

A third student, EC, spoke about how the class changed her outlook on things. "I have a better sense of myself that finally brings me peace. The whole class was about using nature as a destresser, and that is exactly what this class brought me. I've been searching for something to fill this void for a long time, . . . and I think this class helped me close that void. Nature is what I needed to find myself, and I'm so happy I decided to take this class. I learned that I need to involve myself with nature a lot more and receive my daily dose of Nature Rx."[3]

The Arboretum and Public Garden has realized that, at their core, all of its programs are Nature Rx programs. Whether students are learning about the Arboretum collections, doing projects to improve the campus environment, or building leadership skills,

FIGURE 4-2
A UCAPG student engaged in the Learning by Leading program
(Courtesy of Susie Nishio, UC Davis Arboretum and Public Garden)

they are also reaping the health and wellness benefits of being out-side in nature.

University of Minnesota Center for Spirituality and Healing

Founded in 1995, the Earl E. Bakken Center for Spirituality and Healing (CSH) is a multidisciplinary institute offering accredited coursework, graduate degree programs, research efforts, and tar-geted outreach to businesses and organizations. Under the vision-ary leadership of Mary Jo Kreitzer, a professor in the School of Nursing at the University of Minnesota, the center's organizing Wellbeing model is built around six elements:

- health
- relationships
- security
- purpose
- community
- environment

Earl E. Bakken Center for
SPIRITUALITY & HEALING

Mary Jo Kreitzer, PhD, RN, FAAN
© 2012 Regents of the University of Minnesota

FIGURE 4-3

Center for Spirituality and Healing Wellbeing model

(Courtesy of Earl Bakken Center for Spirituality and Healing. Mary Jo Kreitzer, PhD, RN, FAAN. © 2012 Regents of the University of Minnesota)

The CSH is housed within the university's Academic Health Center, while the great majority of its eighty faculty members are based in their own academic departments, except for a few, like Jeannie Larson, whose efforts are split between the CSH and the Minnesota Landscape Arboretum.

Approximately two hundred students take courses through the CSH annually. In an effort to promote nature-based self-care, the CSH teaches graduate-level courses and leads campus-wide initiatives, like the Nature Heals 30x30 pilot in 2015. Nature Heals 30x30 is modeled after the David Suzuki Foundation's 30x30 in Canada, which encourages participants to spend thirty minutes a day in nature for thirty days in a row.[4] Built on a WordPress platform, CSH got three thousand students to participate in the pilot effort. They were sent daily nature notifications over thirty days, with each e-mail suggesting ways in which time in nature is beneficial and offering activities to try. An app was developed to support participants' efforts.

Both prior to and immediately after completing the 30x30 pilot, students completed surveys that measured general well-being, nature-relatedness, and time and type of activities spent in nature-related activities. The questionnaire included a variety of questions pertaining to physical and emotional health derived from the Public Health Surveillance Well-Being Scale (National Center for Health Statistics, 2016) and several questions related to perceived benefits of time spent in nature during participation in the 30x30 events.

From the total participant group, 467 people completed the questionnaires. Participants reported that their lack of participation in outdoor activities was primarily a function of structural factors (weather, time, distance), interpersonal issues (no one to do it with), and safety. Those who responded to postprogram questions had a higher self-rating of well-being and nature connection and spent more time in nature prior to the program than those who did not complete the postprogram survey. Nature-based activities reported by participants in the study were primarily out of doors (as opposed to watching nature-based films, etc.) and involved engagement in exercise or sports activities, although many participants also spent time observing nature or engaging in outdoor events such as concerts or picnics. The least amount of time was spent watching nature-based movies and attending a nature-based lecture. Over 50 percent of individuals were with others at least half of the time they engaged in nature-based activities. While this was a small study, it was encouraging, and in future programs and related studies the focus will be on increasing diverse populations to extend the benefits to more heterogeneous populations.

Like UC Davis, the University of Minnesota embraces all forms of nature-based interactions, from well-designed winter landscapes, to the availability of intramural sports in every season, to encouraging students to visit campus conservatories in the coldest months. Larson says, "We Minnesotans have learned to be creative to sustain ourselves through long winter months—there is a culture of caring about human health and connections to nature throughout the state."[5] Perhaps because of this, the university is very involved with health research and has supported the CSH since its inception.

Larson began her work for the University of Minnesota in 1992 by creating the Horticulture Therapy program at the Arboretum. She has been adding staff to implement nature-based modalities there ever since. In 2012, Larson restructured her program into what is now called Nature-Based Therapeutic services, which offers direct programs, professional training, academic courses, research, and outreach.

Nature-Based Therapeutic services are professionally facilitated interactions with plants, animals, and natural landscapes to bring about measurable outcomes in human health and well-being. Professionally licensed facilitators design, implement, and evaluate custom programs that meet the needs and strengths for a variety of user-group populations.

While the Nature Rx course at UC Davis is intended to provide an overview for undergraduates, Larson's Nature Heals class is for graduate students studying nature-based therapeutics. Topics include restorative environments, therapeutic horticulture, animal-assisted interactions, therapeutic landscapes, forest bathing, green-care farming, facilitated green exercise, wilderness therapy, and ecopsychology. The course provides historic and theoretical perspectives on each of these subjects, along with research into specific techniques and application of techniques to specific populations and settings. Over the course of seven weeks, students' assignments are based on literature application to a given case study, online discussion based on weekly topics, personal nature-based activities, and Pinterest boards. All assignments are meant to combine knowledge and understanding from both a personal and professional point of view.

Parks Research Lab at the College of William and Mary

Dorothy Ibes is an urban human-environment geographer at the College of William and Mary in Williamsburg, Virginia. In her research, Ibes promotes the evolution of healthy, sustainable human settings via parks and public green space.

Ibes directs the Parks Research Lab at William and Mary, through which she initiated the Greater Williamsburg Park Prescription program in 2014. The primary goal of this initiative is to train both campus and community health-care providers to prescribe time outdoors using an online interface. She received inspiration from the groundbreaking work of Robert Zarr, a pediatrician with Unity Health Care (see chapter 3), and financial support from the W&M Environmental Science & Policy Program, the Charles Center, and the Committee on Sustainability. Through this program, Ibes hopes to encourage members of the campus and broader Williamsburg community to spend more time outdoors, ideally by applying the mental health trifecta: being outside, being active, and being social.

After two years of trying to integrate the Park Rx approach into the established medical community on campus, Ibes encountered several hurdles to the success of the program as it was configured. The greatest of these was that trained professionals were enthusiastic about the program but were underutilizing the web portal to prescribe time in nature, usually reporting that they were too rushed to include it in their consultations with patients. This despite the fact that the additional step takes only a few minutes.

In response to this challenge, in the spring of 2016 Ibes decided to reconfigure the traditional Park Rx model, by still providing training and support to health-care providers as needed, but focusing efforts on training Student Park Ambassadors to refer their fellow students to nearby outdoor spaces. This peer-to-peer approach, which bypasses the need to see a professional to obtain a Park Prescription, has proven to be far more effective, leading to a fivefold increase in "referrals" given. During high-stress periods of the semester, students set up tables in heavily trafficked areas; counsel passersby on the best outdoor spaces for their interests, needs, and schedule; and provide a Park Prescription card suggesting a suitable, nearby green space for them to visit. Trained

FIGURE 4-4
Students engaged in the W&M Peer-to-Peer Park Rx program
(Courtesy of William & Mary Parks Research Lab)

student ambassadors also recruit and train the next generation of Student Park Ambassadors, organize other projects around campus to encourage students to get outdoors, and assist Ibes with her research on ecotherapy and barriers to nature connections.

Another project of the Parks Research Lab is a one-credit class titled Campus Park Rx for which students design and implement public space interventions designed to get the campus community outside and help them realize the benefits of nature connections. In 2017, these projects included an outdoor library stocked with nature-themed books; a Community Mandala Day where participants collaboratively created a mandala from natural materials; and social media events such as Green Screen Day (change your device background to a nature image) and Tweet Your Park, during which students provided park prescriptions via Twitter.

The Campus Greenspace Maps, another project of the Parks
Research Lab, is designed to help the campus community get outside. During her first years at William & Mary, Ibes noticed that
many students, especially freshmen, were not familiar with all the
trails and green spaces around campus. This motivated her to seek
funding and enlist the help of student researchers to develop an
interactive map of green spaces on and near campus. The map,
which went live in early 2018, is organized by the user's desired
activity, whether that's hiking, biking, relaxing, eating, or socializing. Users can also rate parks and other outdoor spaces for

different activities, and add comments for other members of the campus community to view.

Nature Rx@Cornell Program

The genesis of the Nature Rx@Cornell program was a meeting several years ago at which a group of faculty members bemoaned the disturbingly high levels of student stress and anxiety at a university renowned for its natural beauty. There should be a way, members of the group thought, of utilizing the green spaces around campus to somehow mitigate the prevalence of psychological problems among the large and diverse student body.

From this initial impetus, the Nature Rx@Cornell program was born. Various professors, staff members, and graduate and undergraduate students were asked to join a steering committee, which brought together representatives from three academic departments, Cornell Botanic Gardens, and the Dean of Students Office, along with the university landscape architect, practitioners from the Cornell Health clinic, the director of Cornell Outdoor Education, and student officers from clubs with a health or wellness focus. Throughout its growth and evolution, the program has depended on the willingness of members of the campus community to donate their time and expertise, and on the dedication displayed by the leader of the initiative.

Early efforts focused on the creation of a Nature Rx app by an information sciences graduate student; a marketing and awareness-raising campaign led by students in the Doris Duke Conservation Scholars program; and a framing of research questions that could lead to better understanding of student needs. Over time, the simple app evolved into a richer and more easily navigated responsive website, naturerx.cornell.edu. The site, designed by Student

Figure 4-6
Home page of the Naturerx.cornell.edu website

Services Information Technology, provides photos and descriptions of fourteen natural and landscaped sites around campus, along with GPS-based walking directions for each site, descriptions of nature-based Cornell groups, and a link to scientific articles on the benefits of time spent in nature. Also linked to this website is a Facebook page for announcing upcoming events and additional resources and an Instagram account for posting photos of activities, natural scenes, and personal experiences.

Over time, the marketing effort has been taken over by the communications team of Cornell Health. They have created a series of "Nature Up" e-posters that extol the virtues of spending time outdoors. These have been displayed on media walls in residential and dining halls and academic buildings, usually in rotation with other notifications of interest to students. The Cornell Health team has also led an effort to encourage instructors to project these posters at the beginning of classes, and many have started to do so.

Spend Time In Nature

Research shows spending quality time in nature is
good for your overall health and well-being.

Recommendations

Take a walk or run around Beebe Lake,
rest on the Slope, enjoy a sunset, etc.

Recommended dosage

Approximately 20 minutes, 2–3 times a week

 ature Rx
@Cornell _____

signature of Cornell Health provider

If symptoms worsen, visit *health.cornell.edu* or call 607-255-5155 for consultation.

FIGURE 4-7
A Cornell Health nature prescription

One of the major advances for the Nature Rx@Cornell program has been the introduction by Cornell Health of a nature prescription program. Modeled after the Park Rx America program described in chapter 3, this effort has involved physicians and clinicians providing students with a Spend Time in Nature paper prescription as part of their overall health plan. In the 2017–18 academic year, over 250 nature prescriptions were provided to students.

Because of confidentiality restrictions, it's difficult to quantify what percentage of the students handed these prescriptions actually follow up by spending time in nature, nor is it possible to determine the degree to which nature has improved their underlying conditions. What is known is that through the various publicity efforts and the use of nature prescriptions, student awareness of the benefits of spending time in nature has greatly increased at Cornell. In a recent survey of undergraduates at the university, as many respondents said that they had heard of Nature Rx@Cornell as those who had not. We now hope to reach a longer-term goal of having all students include quality outdoor time as part of their daily routine.

Since the Nature Rx@Cornell initiative is aimed at the student body, it became clear to the steering committee that undergraduates needed to become more directly involved. Thus in the fall of 2017, a group of students came together to form the Nature Rx Club. As of this writing, activities sponsored by the Nature Rx Club have included weekly walks through natural and garden areas on campus; tabling at campus-wide events such as ECO Fest and the Student Farmer's Market; and sponsoring of special events, such as a talk on how to dress for the cold or a winter tour of the tropical conservatory (se appendix B).

A particularly laudable approach taken by the leaders of the Nature Rx Club has been their outreach to groups that are normally underrepresented in outdoor activities. These have included students from Hawaii and other tropical zones, many of whom have trouble adjusting to the cold of an upstate New York winter; African American and Latino/Latina students, many of whom are from urban backgrounds; and students with physical disabilities. To convey a sense of inclusiveness, the group is using taglines such as "Time in Nature = A Healthier You" and "There Is No Bad Weather, Only Inappropriate Dress." Student leaders are also contributing to the marketing effort by developing quarter cards (leaflets comprising one-quarter of a standard-size sheet of paper) and clothing with the Nature Rx@Cornell logo.

As with any start-up programs, not all efforts made under the Nature Rx@Cornell umbrella have been successful. An attempt to create a Take It Outside class for first-year students, in which a variety of campus experts would lead students on walks through a different natural area each week, did not meet enrollment expectations and has been shelved until a more effective promotional approach can be identified. Also, the Nature Rx Club has experienced growing pains, with some offerings much better attended than others. Rather than viewing these as failures, the steering committee is treating them as learning experiences and analyzing ways to make them more successful in the future.

The early impetus to engage in research that would provide new insights on how time spent in nature can contribute to young people's well-being has spurred the development of partnerships between faculty members across units at Cornell and beyond. A systematic review that focused on the question "What is the minimum time dose in nature to positively impact the mental health of college-aged youth?" was conducted by experts from Horticulture, Public Health, Cornell Libraries, and Design and Environmental Analysis. Another project, which surveyed Cornell undergraduates about the relationship between their interaction with nature in their middle childhood years and their engagement with and attitudes toward nature today was also led by faculty from two colleges. A third, not yet under way as of this writing, features a collaboration between faculty at Cornell and the College of William and Mary.

Other Nature-Oriented Efforts at Cornell

It is important to point out that not all efforts at Cornell intended to get students to spend time in and appreciate nature are formally part of Nature Rx@Cornell. Marcia Eames-Sheavly is a senior lecturer in the Section of Horticulture and offers such courses as The Art of Horticulture, Plants and Human Well-Being, Botanical Illustration, and Healing Plants and the People Who Use Them. Eames-Sheavly is greatly troubled by the busyness or mindless racing of so many students today, and cites the statistic that Cornell has been rated as one of the twenty-five most stressful colleges in the United States. In her fourteen years of teaching, she observes that students seem increasingly risk averse, and are much more anxious with more mental health problems. She also feels that students are less present in their lives, and blames this on the dependence on electronic technology, which causes their different daily activities to all blend together.

In an attempt to combat these trends, Eames-Sheavly assigns students in her various classes to spend an hour "slowing down and looking up." Depending on the course, students turn in either journal entries, art projects, or poems based on their nature inter- actions. But altering undergraduate mind-sets isn't easy, as Eames-Sheavly has shared: "Asking students to step outside as a class and make observations, as we did two weeks ago, gathering at the base of a walnut tree, is a challenge. Despite having several clear guide- lines for noticing, writing, and looking up some material, in a critical incident questionnaire distributed at the end of class, some talked about feeling 'restless and bored' with standing outside."[6] Clearly, more work needs to be done.

Yet another innovative approach is offered by Cornell Botanic Gardens as a series of weekly walks under the title of Mindful Bot- any: "Join Cornell Botanic Gardens staff to observe the beauty of spring unfurl on weekly spring nature walks. While following the same route each week, we will practice mindfulness by dedicat- ing our attention to the present moment and fully observing the amazing transformations that take place during spring."[7] This series is open to everyone in the Cornell community and beyond, but the Nature Rx Club is promoting the walks in hopes of attracting students to participate.

Finally, Cornell, like many institutions, offers a program in outdoor education. Cornell Outdoor Education has a mission to develop students' teamwork and leadership skills and inner growth through outdoor experiences. They offer over 130 courses each year with a total enrollment of more than twenty thousand.[8] One can assume that these student enrollees gain a tremendous appreciation for nature through these courses. But it's also fair to conclude that the program has trouble attracting those most resistant to spending time in the natural world.

From the descriptions of the programs at these four institutions of higher learning, certain conclusions can be reached. The first is that US undergraduates, whether at large Ivy League universities or smaller southern colleges, are experiencing unprecedented levels of stress, anxiety, and related psychological problems. The second is that each school, even the most urban ones, offer green spaces on or near campus in which students can be encouraged to spend time and unwind. A third is that there are many different approaches to Nature Rx programs, and that the approach taken by a particular institution should build on its unique strengths. In the next chapter, we expand on these general conclusions to explore the potential growth of Nature Rx programs on US campuses; how such programs might impact environmental attitudes among participating students; and what such programs say about the future of the residential university in the United States.

5

The Role of Nature Rx Programs in the Future of Higher Education

Limitations or Barriers to Creating Nature Rx Programs

An impression may have been created in the previous chapters that it is relatively simple to create a Nature Rx program on a college or university campus, and that all institutions are equally able to accommodate such an approach. However, neither of these impressions is universally true.

Schools that are primarily or exclusively residential rather than commuter-based can focus on all aspects of their students' lives, rather than just while they are taking classes. But commuter-based institutions, which include the majority of community colleges, rarely see their students overnight or on weekends. It can therefore be far more difficult for counselors at these schools to identify individual students' psychological challenges and to enact nature-based programs that aim to alleviate those conditions. In addition, commuting students are far less likely to perceive their campuses as places to heal whatever is plaguing them.

While the argument was raised in an earlier chapter that even the most urban campuses have some green spaces to which students can retreat, it is also true that many city-based universities depend on nearby parks to provide that connection with nature. At NYU in Greenwich Village, New York, Washington Square Park is the de facto green space for students and the locale for many wellness activities. Similarly, students at the University of Chicago can cross Cottage Grove Avenue to access the green Hyde Park complex. But given that these parks are not under the control of the nearby academic institutions, it would be challenging to base Nature Rx–like programs in those locations.

Local climate can certainly be another limiting factor, as institutions in the northern tier of the United States and through much of Canada experience lengthy winter periods that may discourage spending time in nature. Conversely, southern colleges and universities can be sweltering in the late spring, and students may be reluctant to leave air-conditioned buildings. But as described in chapter 3, the key to overcoming these weather-related challenges is to teach students how to dress for each season and to customize events based on current conditions.

Beyond these more obvious limitations, however, an institution interested in establishing a Nature Rx program must demonstrate a commitment to utilizing whatever natural sites are available to contribute to students' well-being. If a college or university holds academics or athletics or research agendas as singularly paramount and are less focused on student well-being, then Nature Rx programs will probably never flourish.

The institution must also recognize that, while Nature Rx programs are not expensive, they do require a commitment from many undergraduate and graduate students and a variety of campus personnel, including faculty members and staff from units as disparate as the health clinic, student services, landscape architect, and marketing. Coordinating all of their efforts into a unified program can be a substantial undertaking for whoever volunteers for or is assigned this task. An assessment needs to be conducted of how this assignment would fit into that individual's other responsibilities.

A final challenge to employing nature as a campus-healing tool can be the student body itself. While the student population at a particular college or university is never homogeneous, it is also true that some schools have a reputation for excessive student partying, while others are known for obsessively academically oriented individuals who strive for the best possible grades. The creation of a Nature Rx program depends on having a core of students who are committed to a balance in life, between their classes, recreational, and discretionary activities.

How Can the Effectiveness of a Nature Rx Program Be Evaluated?

Before an academic institution can evaluate the effectiveness of a programmatic effort, it must establish exactly what goals it is hoping the program will achieve, so that metrics can be identified to measure progress toward those goals. In the case of Nature Rx programs, one overarching goal may be to improve the overall well-being of the student body. If the health clinic is able to release data on the number of students visiting for psychological counseling, this could be a valuable metric to trace over the course of the program. Another goal may be to increase environmental awareness among students, in which case an attitude-focused survey of students may be the correct tool for assessing success. Even a reduction in the incidence of binge drinking or illicit drug use can be a worthy goal, which can be assessed by studying the number of students requiring medical treatments as a result of such behavior both before and after the introduction of the program.

Since both qualitative and quantitative data can contribute to program evaluation, it can also be useful to ask residence hall directors or residence assistants to keep logs of the number of students under their purview who come to them with psychologically oriented troubles. While this more anecdotal feedback may be less scientifically rigorous, it can still provide insights into whether the Nature Rx programming efforts are having an impact.

Many institutions of higher learning are now embracing large-scale sustainability goals, and it's worth examining how a Nature Rx program supports a campus's sustainability agenda. There is evidence that young people who spend time in nature are more likely to adopt an environmental focus,[1] so engaging in a Nature Rx program may result in students who adopt more environmentally sensitive lifestyles and advocate for the college's sustainability agenda. This too can be quantified by identifying the number of ecologically oriented student-led groups that develop after the Nature Rx program is initiated.

Whatever metrics are used to evaluate the effectiveness of a Nature Rx program, it's important that adequate time passes before measuring change. Human behavior changes slowly, and college-aged students are confronted daily with a multiplicity of choices. Provide a long enough duration for the program to become part of the university culture before assessing its effectiveness.

The Role of Nature Rx Programs in the Future of Higher Education

In his book *The Creation of the Future: The Role of the American University*, Frank H.T. Rhodes, a professor emeritus of geology and former president of Cornell, advances the argument that "the centuries-old monopoly on education enjoyed by universities is over, a casualty to other means of learning (information technology and the internet) and other providers (especially corporate America and for-profit vendors)." He goes on to say that "the traditional pattern of learning—by college-age students enrolled full-time in a residential, rigidly sequential program—is being replaced by on-demand, anytime, and often on-line learning from an increasingly competitive 'Knowledge business.'"[2]

Rather than despairing, however, Rhodes then lays out a series of steps that universities can take to regain their essential educational role. He argues that the greatest strength of institutions of higher learning is the structure of community that they provide: "The effective university depends on community, because the interacting community multiplies the power and extends the reach of its members."[3]

In the fractious and often divisive times in which we live, a university campus that includes a celebration of the natural environment can provide a sense of community inclusive of various political, social, and ethnic backgrounds and orientations. A sense of belonging to a community can go a long way toward overcoming the isolation that often accompanies a college experience.

From a student's perspective, a college or university is a demanding environment: it demands intellectual rigor to succeed in classes, an introspection to determine where one best fits socially, and rigorous time management to accommodate all of one's daily needs. In a word, it can be exhausting. The college or university has an obligation to provide an environment that nurtures the whole person. As Stephen Lau and Feng Yang have said, "To protect and maintain the health of university students, who would be the future pillars of our society, it is important to promote a health-supportive and sustainable campus environment."[4]

Nature can provide some fundamental lessons to help students struggling to cope with multiple demands. Sitting quietly in a woodland, one is made aware of the competing forces of cooperation and competition that are ever present in the natural world. Similarly, each college student engages in both cooperative activities (joint project research, group study sessions) as well as competitive ones (everything from varsity athletics and ultimate

Frisbee games to fellowship applications and student government elections). The seasonal changes in that woodland also help students appreciate the larger natural forces that they are part of, which can go a long way toward putting a low grade on a single exam into a manageable perspective.

Nature can also be thought of as the great healer, its setting shown to reduce stress, blood pressure, and heart rate, and increase memory recall and mental acuity. There is now an overwhelming body of evidence that spending time in nature leads to healthier individuals (see chapter 2).

The green spaces around a campus can also serve as living classrooms for the consideration of varying viewpoints on such heated issues as best use of natural resources, mitigation of climate change, and the role of the university in affecting policy. Somehow, no issue seems as contentious when group members are sitting around a campfire in the woods.

The establishment of authentic community cannot be achieved through an online institution, even given the ubiquity of social media communication. A physical presence, in which individuals engage in dialogue, however heated, is what is needed to increase understanding and to build bridges between people.

Envisioning a Brighter Future

The primary functions typically associated with colleges and universities are academics, research, athletics, and perhaps outreach. But what if this list expanded to include the health and well-being of all members of the community: students, faculty, and staff? And what if one of the essential approaches to achieving this community-wide wellness was through an emphasis on time outdoors in nature?

There is sufficient concern today about the high incidence of both physical and psychological problems among students that college and university administrators and health-care providers are focusing increasingly on how to reverse these trends. Counseling, the prescribing of pharmaceuticals, peer-to-peer interventions, and awareness campaigns all play important roles. But where do Nature Rx programs fit into the mix?

As strongly as we have advocated in this book for having students spend time in nature, we recognize that it is just one component of addressing student health. Of equal importance is having students adopt an overall healthy lifestyle. Individuals who commit to nature interludes, coupled with a sensible diet, regular exercise, good sleep patterns, and effective work-life balance, often exhibit increased resistance to illnesses, resilience in the face of setbacks, greater energy levels, and more positive moods.

In a college or university setting, the most effective way to get students to adopt such healthy choices is for the adults in their lives to model the behavior. While it is beyond the purview of this book to address the inherent stresses wrought by the tenure review system or by overly heavy caseloads of health professionals, all members of a campus community can commit to spending ten to fifteen minutes a few times per week on a nature walk; to eating a diet high in fibers and low in fats and sugar; and to balancing their work time with activities that are personally gratifying.

Colleges and universities are often referred to as institutions of higher learning. We envision a time when an inherent component of that higher learning will involve communities of individuals united by a love of nature, exploring their own and the society's betterment.

Appendix A

UC Davis Arboretum and Public Garden Nature Rx Course Syllabus

Description: The student experience can be demanding, and learning how to balance it all can be complicated. Fortunately, finding relief can sometimes be as easy as walking out the door and into nature. Multiple studies have shown that spending time in nature improves health and well-being and reduces stress and anxiety. This seminar aims to introduce you to some of the living landscapes of UC Davis, from the Arboretum to the Student Farm to the Putah Creek Riparian Reserve, to learn what makes them unique and to enjoy their inherent beauty. Through walks, bike rides, painting adventures, and guided tours, we'll discover the wonders of the natural world around us.

Learning Outcomes:

- Become familiar with faculty, staff, and other students at UC Davis
- Become acquainted with the location of gardens, the Arboretum, and natural areas of UC Davis and how to access them
- Understand the therapeutic benefits associated with spending time in nature and the ways in which it can benefit your sense of well-being
- Identify the organizations that can help you stay connected to nature throughout your tenure at UC Davis

- Reflect on the value of nature to your well-being during your time at UC Davis

Schedule:

Date	Topic/Activity	Guest speaker(s)
9/22	Nature Rx introduction	Stacey Parker, Haven Kiers
9/29	Watercolor walk	Chip Sullivan
10/6	Student Farm	Carol Hillhouse, Raoul Adamchak
10/13	Campus tree walk	Jim Harding
10/20	Forest bathing	Rose Lawrence
10/27	Ecology of Putah Creek	Peter Moyle
11/3	CA native plants	Stew Winchester
11/10	Gratitude garden walk	Wellness Ambassadors
11/17	Land art	Liz Boults

Appendix B

Cornell Nature Rx Club:
Spring Activities

4/12 THRIVE with Nature

- Self-care techniques with nature
- Build resilience and practice mindfulness walking

4/20 Art of Ag Day

- Arts Quad: create woven tapestries with natural materials
- Ag Quad: make paper with natural dyes

4/20 Spa Night

- Labyrinth of plants and taking succulent cuttings
- Informative fliers with plant care information
- Informative fliers on research demonstrating nature's benefits

4/29 Meteor Shower Observations

- Nighttime viewing from the Fuertes Observatory

5/4 Weed and munch at the Willard Straight Rock Garden

- Help restore this historic garden and snack on vegan nachos

5/12   Cornell Botanic Gardens Tour

- In collaboration with Cornell Botanic Gardens and Cornell Minds Matter

Notes

1. The Mental Health Crisis on US Campuses

1. Kevin Eagan, et al., *The American Freshman: National Norms Fall 2015* (Los Angeles: Higher Education Research Institute, UCLA, 2017).

2. American College Health Association, *American College Health Association–National College Health Assessment II: Reference Group Executive Summary Spring 2016* (Hanover, MD: American College Health Association, 2016).

3. Center for Collegiate Mental Health, *2016 Annual Report* (Penn State University, publication no. STA 17–74, 2017).

4. Ibid.

5. *The Association for University and College Counseling Center Directors Annual Survey*, 2016, accessed March 27, 2018, https://www.aucccd.org/assets/documents/aucccd%202016%20monograph%20-%20public.pdf.

6. Jean M. Twenge, *Generation Me: Why Today's Young Americans Are More Confident, Assertive, Entitled—and More Miserable Than Ever Before* (New York: Atria Paperback, 2014).

7. Sampathirao Prabhakararao, "Overuse of Social Media Affects the Mental Health of Adolescents and Early Youth," *International Journal of Indian Psychiatry* 3, no. 2 (2016): 14–19.

8. M. Dooris, "The University as a Setting for Sustainable Health: University of Central Lancashire," in *Health Promoting Universities: Concept, Experience and Framework for Action*, ed. A.D. Tsouros, G. Dowding, J. Thompson, and M. Dooris, 105–20 (Copenhagen: World Health Organization, Regional Office for Europe, 1998).

9. S. Abelson and Greg T. Eells, "Promoting and Protecting Student Health," *NASPA Leadership Exchange*, Winter 2016, 14–20.

10. Ibid.

11. Janis Whitlock, "Self-Injurious Behavior in Adolescents," *PLoS Med* 7, no. 5 (2010): e1000240. https://doi.org/10.1371/journal.pmed.1000240.

12. Allan J. Schwartz, "College Student Suicide in the United States: 1990–1991 through 2003–2004," *Journal of American College Health* 54, no. 6 (2006): 341–52.

13. International Association of Counseling Services, *Standards for University and College Counseling Services*, 2016, https://0201.nccdn.net/4_2/000/000/053/0e8/2017-STANDARDS-10-5-17.pdf.

14. Philip W. Meilman and Tanni M. Hall, "Aftermath of Tragic Events: The Development and Use of Community Support Meetings on a University Campus," *Journal of American College Health* 54, no. 6 (2006): 382–84.

15. "Means Matter," Harvard T.H. Chan School of Public Health, accessed February 13, 2018, https://www.hsph.harvard.edu/means-matter.

2. The Proven Benefits of Spending Time in Nature

1. James G. Lennox, *Aristotle: On the Parts of Animals I–IV*, Oxford: Oxford University Press, 2001.

2. Ralph W. Emerson, *Nature*, Boston: James Munro, 1836.

3. John Muir, *Our National Parks*, Boston: Houghton Mifflin, 1901.

4. Rachel Carson, *Silent Spring*, New York: Houghton Mifflin, 1962.

5. Stephen Kaplan, "The Restorative Benefits of Nature: Toward an Integrative Framework," *Journal of Environmental Psychology* 15 (1995): 169–82; Stephen Kaplan and Rachel Kaplan, *The Experience of Nature* (New York: Cambridge University Press, 1989).

6. Terry Hartig et al., "Tracking Restoration in Natural and Urban Field Settings," *Journal of Environmental Psychology* 23 (2003): 109–23.

7. Ruth Ann Atchley, David L. Strayer, and Paul Atchley, "Creativity in the Wild: Improving Creative Reasoning through Immersion in Natural Settings," *PLOS One* 7, no. 12 (2012): 1–3.

8. Roger S. Ulrich et al., "Stress Recovery during Exposure to Natural and Urban Environments," *Journal of Environmental Psychology* 11, no. 3 (1991): 201–30.

9. Bum Jin Park et al., "The Physiological Effects of 'Shinrin-yoku' (Taking in the Forest Atmosphere or Forest Bathing): Evidence from Field Experiments in 24 Forests across Japan," *Environmental Health and Preventive Medicine* 15 (2010): 18–26.

10. Chorong Song et al., "Physiological and Psychological Responses of Young Males during Spring-Time Walks in Urban Parks," *Journal of Physiological Anthropology* 33, no. 1 (2014): 1–8.

11. Gregory N. Bratman et al., "Nature Experience Reduces Rumination and Subgenual Prefrontal Cortex Activation," *PNAS* 112, no. 28 (2015): 8567–72.

12. Ulrika K. Stigsdotter et al., "Nature-Based Therapeutic Interventions," in *Forest, Trees, and Human Health*, ed. Kjell Nilsson et al., chapter 11 (Amsterdam: Springer Link, 2011).

13. Alan Ewert and Aiko Yoshino, "The Influence of Short-Term Adventure-Based Experiences on Levels of Resilience," *Journal of Adventure Education and Outdoor Learning* 11, no. 1 (2011): 35–50.

14. Bratman et al., "Nature Experience Reduces Rumination."

15. Ewert and Yoshino, "Influence of Short-Term Adventure-Based Experiences."

16. Johan Ottosson and Patrik Grahn, "The Role of Natural Settings in Crisis Rehabilitation," *Landscape Restoration* 33 (2008): 51–70.

17. Marc G. Berman et al., "Interacting with Nature Improves Cognition and Affect for Individuals with Depression," *Journal of Affective Disorders* 140, no. 3 (2012): 300–305.

18. Mardie M. Townsend, Cecily Pryor, and Anita Field, "Health and Well-Being Naturally: 'Contact with Nature' in Health Promotion for Targeted Individuals, Communities, and Populations," *Health Promotion Journal of Australia* 17, no. 2 (2006): 114–23.

19. Kaplan, "Restorative Benefits of Nature."

20. A.L. McFarland, T.M. Waliczek, and J.M. Zajicek, "The Relationship between Student Use of Campus Green Spaces and Perceptions of Quality of Life," *HortTechnology* 18, no. 2 (2008): 232–38.

21. Janet Speake, Sally Edmondson, and Haq Nawaz, "Everyday Encounters with Nature: Students' Perceptions and Use of University Campus Green Spaces," *Human Geographies* 7, no. 1 (2013): 21–31.

22. Roger S. Ulrich, "Human Responses to Vegetation and Landscapes," *Landscape and Urban Planning* 12 (1986): 29–44.

23. Carolyn M. Tennessen and Bernadine Cimprich, "Views of Nature: Effects on Attention," *Journal of Environmental Psychology* 15 (1995): 77–85.

24. Gary Felsten, "Where to Take a Study Break on the College Campus: An Attention Restoration Theory Perspective," *Journal of Environmental Psychology* 29 (2009): 160–67.

25. Tammy Kohlleppel, Jennifer Campbell Bradley, and Steve Jacob, "A Walk through the Garden: Can a Visit to a Botanic Garden Reduce Stress?" *HortTechnology* 12, no. 3 (2002): 489–92.

26. Christopher L. Wassenberg, Marni A. Goldenberg, and Katherine E. Soule, "Benefits of Botanical Garden Visitation: A Means-End Study," *Urban Forestry and Urban Greening* 14 (2015): 148–55.

27. Agnes E. Van Den Berg and Mariette H.G. Custers, "Gardening Promotes Neuroendocrine and Affective Restoration from Stress," *Journal of Health Psychology* 16, no. 1 (2011): 3–11.

28. Jane Clatworthy, Joe Hinds, and Paul M. Camic, "Gardening as a Mental Health Intervention: A Review." *Mental Health Review Journal* 18, no. 4 (2013): 214–25; Agnes E. Van den Berg et al., "Allotment Gardening and Health: A Comparative Survey among Allotment Gardeners and Their Neighbors without an Allotment," *Environmental Health* 9 (2010): 74.

29. Cynthia L. Ogden et al., "Trends in Obesity Prevalence among Children and Adolescents in the United States, 1988–1994 through 2013–2014," *JAMA* 315, no. 21 (2016): 2292–99.

30. Victoria J. Rideout, Ulla G. Foehr, and Donald F. Roberts, *Generation M2: Media in the Lives of 8- to 18-Year-Olds*, Menlo Park, CA: Henry J. Kaiser Family Foundation, 2010.

31. Physical Activity Council, *2017 Participation Report: The Physical Activity Council's Annual Report Tracking Sports, Fitness, and Recreation Participation in the US*, http://physicalactivitycouncil.com/PDFs/current.pdf, 2017.

32. Outdoor Foundation, *Outdoor Recreation Report 2013*, https://outdoor industry.org/wp-content/uploads/2017/05/2013-Outdoor-ResearchParticipation1. pdf.

33. Qing Li et al., "Acute Effects of Walking in Forest Environments on Cardiovascular and Metabolic Parameters," *European Journal of Applied Physiology* 111, no. 11 (2011): 2845–53; Qing Li et al., "Effect of Phytoncide from Trees on Human Natural Killer Cell Function," *International Journal of Immunopathology and Pharmacology* 22 (2009): 951–59; Samantha Dayawansa et al., "Autonomic Responses during Inhalation of Natural Fragrance of 'Cedrol' in Humans," *Autonomic Neuroscience* 108 (2003): 79–86.

34. Christopher A. Lowry et al., "Identification of an Immune-Responsive Mesolimbocortical Serotonergic System: Potential Role in Regulation of Emotional Behavior," *Neuroscience* 146, no. 2 (2007): 756–72.

35. Dorothy Matthews and Susan Jenks, "Can Bacteria Make You Smarter?," *AAAS EurekAlert*, May 24, 2010, https://www.eurekalert.org/pub_releases/ 2010-05/asfm-cbm052010.php.

36. Ming Kuo, "How Might Contact with Nature Promote Human Health? Promising Mechanisms and a Possible Central Pathway," *Frontiers in Psychology* 6 (2015): 1–8, doi:10.3389/fpsyg.2015.01093.

37. Qing Li et al., "Forest Bathing Enhances Human Natural Killer Activity and Expression of Anti-Cancer Proteins," *International Journal of Immunopathology and Pharmacology* 20 (2007): 3–8.

38. Qing Li, et al., "A Forest Bathing Trip Increases Human Natural Killer Activity and Expression of Anti-Cancer Proteins in Female Subjects," *Journal of Biological Regulators and Homeostatic Agents* 22, no. 1 (2008): 45–55.

39. Jeanette E. Boudreau and Katharine C. Hsu, "Natural Killer Cells in Human Health and Disease," *Current Opinion in Immunology* 50 (2018): 102–11.

40. Matthew J. Sheetz and George L. King, "Molecular Understanding of Hyperglycemia's Adverse Effects for Diabetic Complications," *JAMA* 288 (2002): 2579–88.

41. Kuo, "How Might Contact with Nature Promote Human Health?"

42. Jo Barton and Jules Pretty, "What Is the Best Dose of Nature and Green Exercise for Improving Mental Health? A Multi-Study Analysis," *Environmental Science and Technology* 44 (2010): 3947–55.

43. MaryCarol Hunter, e-mail message to author, July 7, 2017.

3. Developing a Nature Rx Program on a College Campus

1. Robert Zarr, Linda Cottrell, and Chaya Merrill, "Park Prescription (DC Park Rx): A New Strategy to Combat Chronic Disease in Children," *Journal of Physical Activity and Health* 14 (2017): 1–2.

2. Park Rx America, accessed September 20, 2017, https://parkrxamerica.org/about.php.

3. "Docs in the Park Program," Department of Recreation and Parks, City of Baltimore, accessed September 20, 2017, https://bcrp.baltimorecity.gov/special-programs/docs.

4. LiveWell Greenville, accessed September 20, 2017, https://livewellgreenville.org/community-action/?select-action=at-play-2.

5. Jeannie Larson, personal communication, September 4, 2017.

4. Nature Rx Programs on Four University Campuses

1. Online Etymology Dictionary, s.v. "campus," accessed October 17, 2017, http://www.etymonline.com/word/campus.

2. Janice C. Griffith, "Open Space Preservation: An Imperative for Quality Campus Environments," *Journal of Higher Education* 65, no. 6 (1994): 645–69.

3. Interviews with UC Davis students, April 17, 2017.

4. "The One Nature Challenge," David Suzuki Foundation, accessed August 7, 2018, https://davidsuzuki.org/take-action/act-locally/one-nature-challenge/?nabe=5392362493968384:1&utm_referrer=https%3A%2F%2Fwww.google.com%2F.

5. Jeannie Larson, personal communication, September 4, 2017.

6. Marcia Eames-Sheavly, personal communication, November 13, 2017.

7. "Learning at Cornell Botanic Gardens," Cornell Botanic Gardens, accessed February 14, 2018, http://www.cornellbotanicgardens.org/learning.

8. Cornell Outdoor Education, accessed March 9, 2018, https://coe.cornell.edu/about-coe.

5. The Role of Nature Rx Programs in the Future of Higher Education

1. Laurie P. Browne, Barry A. Garst, and M. Deborah Bialeschki, "Engaging Youth in Environmental Sustainability: Impact of the Camp 2 Grow Program," *Journal of Park and Recreation Administration* 29, no. 3 (2011): 70–85.

2. Frank H.T. Rhodes, *The Creation of the Future: The Role of the American University* (Ithaca, NY: Cornell University Press, 2001).

3. Ibid.

4. Stephen S.Y. Lau and Feng Yang, "Introducing Healing Gardens into a Compact University Campus: Design Natural Space to Create Healthy and Sustainable Campuses," *Landscape Research* 34, no. 1 (2009): 55–81.

Bibliography

Abelson, S., and Greg T. Eells. "Promoting and Protecting Student Health." *NASPA Leadership Exchange*, Winter 2016, 14–20.

American College Health Association. *American College Health Association-National College Health Assessment II: Reference Group Executive Summary Spring 2016*. Hanover, MD: American College Health Association, 2016.

The Association for University and College Counseling Center Directors Annual Survey. 2016. Accessed March 27, 2018. https://www.aucccd.org/assets/documents/aucccd%202016%20monograph%20-%20public.pdf.

Atchley, Ruth Ann, David L. Strayer, and Paul Atchley. "Creativity in the Wild: Improving Creative Reasoning through Immersion in Natural Settings." *PLOS One* 7, no. 12 (2012): 1–3.

Barton, Jo, and Jules Pretty. "What Is the Best Dose of Nature and Green Exercise for Improving Mental Health? A Multi-Study Analysis." *Environmental Science and Technology* 44 (2010): 3947–55.

Berman, Marc G., Ethan Kross, Katherine M. Krpan, Mary K. Askren, Aleah Burson, Patricia J. Deldin, Stephen Kaplan, Lindsey Sherdell, Ian H. Gotlib, and John Jonides. "Interacting with Nature Improves Cognition and Affect for Individuals with Depression." *Journal of Affective Disorders* 140, no. 3 (2012): 300–305.

Boudreau, Jeanette E., and Katharine C. Hsu. "Natural Killer Cells in Human Health and Disease." *Current Opinion in Immunology* 50 (2018): 102–11.

Bratman, Gregory N., J. Paul Hamilton, Kevin S. Hahn, Gretchen C. Daly, and James J. Gross. "Nature Experience Reduces Rumination and Subgenual Prefrontal Cortex Activation." *PNAS* 112, no. 28 (2015): 8567–72.

Browne, Laurie P., Barry A. Garst, and M. Deborah Bialeschki. "Engaging Youth in Environmental Sustainability: Impact of the Camp2Grow Program." *Journal of Park and Recreation Administration* 29, no. 3 (2011): 70–85.

Carson, Rachel. *Silent Spring*. New York: Houghton Mifflin, 1962.

Center for Collegiate Mental Health. *2016 Annual Report*. Penn State University, publication no. STA 17–74. 2017.

Clatworthy, Jane, Joe Hinds, and Paul M. Camic. "Gardening as a Mental Health Intervention: A Review." *Mental Health Review Journal* 18, no. 4 (2013): 214–25.

Cornell Outdoor Education. Accessed March 9, 2018. https://coe.cornell.edu/about-coe.

Dayawansa, Samantha, K. Umeno, H. Takakura, E. Hori, E. Tabuchi, Y. Nagashima, T. Suzuki, T. Ono, and H. Nishijo. "Autonomic Responses during Inhalation of Natural Fragrance of 'Cedrol' in Humans." *Autonomic Neuroscience* 108 (2003): 79–86.

"Docs in the Park Program." Department of Recreation and Parks. City of Baltimore. Accessed September 20, 2017. https://bcrp.baltimorecity.gov/special-programs/docs.

Dooris, M. "The University as a Setting for Sustainable Health: University of Central Lancashire." In *Health Promoting Universities: Concept, Experience and Framework for Action*, edited by A.D. Tsouros, G. Dowding, J. Thompson, and M. Dooris, 105–20. Copenhagen: World Health Organization, Regional Office for Europe, 1998.

Eagan, Kevin, Ellen Bara Stolzenberg, Abigail K. Bates, Melissa C. Aragon, Maria Ramirez Suchard, and Cecilia Rios-Aguilar. *The American Freshman: National Norms Fall 2015*. Los Angeles: Higher Education Research Institute, UCLA, 2017.

Emerson, Ralph W. *Nature*. Boston: James Munro, 1836.

Ewert, Alan, and Aiko Yoshino. "The Influence of Short-Term Adventure-Based Experiences on Levels of Resilience." *Journal of Adventure Education and Outdoor Learning* 11, no. 1 (2011): 35–50.

Felsten, Gary. "Where to Take a Study Break on the College Campus: An Attention Restoration Theory Perspective." *Journal of Environmental Psychology* 29 (2009): 160–67.

Griffith, Janice C. "Open Space Preservation: An Imperative for Quality Campus Environments." *Journal of Higher Education* 65, no. 6 (1994): 645–69.

Hartig, Terry, Gary W. Evans, Larry D. Jamner, Deborah S. Davis, and Tommy Gärling. "Tracking Restoration in Natural and Urban Field Settings." *Journal of Environmental Psychology* 23 (2003): 109–23.

International Association of Counseling Services. *Standards for University and College Counseling Services*. 2016. https://0201.nccdn.net/4_2/000/000/053/0e8/2017-STANDARDS-10-5-17.pdf.

Kaplan, Stephen. "The Restorative Benefits of Nature: Toward an Integrative Framework." *Journal of Environmental Psychology* 15 (1995): 169–82.

Kaplan, Stephen, and Rachel Kaplan. *The Experience of Nature.* New York: Cambridge University Press, 1989.

Kohlleppel, Tammy, Jennifer Campbell Bradley, and Steve Jacob. "A Walk through the Garden: Can a Visit to a Botanic Garden Reduce Stress?" *HortTechnology* 12, no. 3 (2002): 489–92.

Kuo, Ming. "How Might Contact with Nature Promote Human Health? Promising Mechanisms and a Possible Central Pathway." *Frontiers in Psychology* 6 (2015): 1–8. doi:10.3389/fpsyg.2015.01093.

Lau, Stephen S.Y., and Feng Yang. "Introducing Healing Gardens into a Compact University Campus: Design Natural Space to Create Healthy and Sustainable Campuses." *Landscape Research* 34, no. 1 (2009): 55–81.

"Learning at Cornell Botanic Gardens." Cornell Botanic Gardens. Accessed February 14, 2018. http://www.cornellbotanicgardens.org/learning.

Lennox, James G. *Aristotle: On the Parts of Animals I–IV.* Oxford: Oxford University Press, 2001.

Li, Qing, M. Kobayashi, Y. Wakayama, H. Inagaki, M. Katsumata, Y. Hirata, K. Hirata et al. "Effect of Phytoncide from Trees on Human Natural Killer Cell Function." *International Journal of Immunopathology and Pharmacology* 22 (2009): 951–59.

Li, Qing, K. Morimoto, A. Nakadai, H. Inagaki, M. Katsumata, T. Shimizu, Y. Hirata et al. "Forest Bathing Enhances Human Natural Killer Activity and Expression of Anti-Cancer Proteins." *International Journal of Immunopathology and Pharmacology* 20 (2007): 3–8.

Li, Qing, Kanehisa Morimoto, M. Kobayashi, and Y. Miyazaki. "A Forest Bathing Trip Increases Human Natural Killer Activity and Expression of Anti-Cancer Proteins in Female Subjects." *Journal of Biological Regulators and Homeostatic Agents* 22, no. 1 (2008): 45–55.

Li, Qing, Toshiaki Otsuka, Maiko Kobayashi, Yoko Wakayama, Hirofumi Inagaki, Masao Katsumata, Yukiyo Hirata et al. "Acute Effects of Walking in Forest Environments on Cardiovascular and Metabolic Parameters." *European Journal of Applied Physiology* 111, no. 11 (2011): 2845–53.

LiveWell Greenville. Accessed September 20, 2017. https://livewellgreenville. org/community-action/?select-action=at-play-2.

Lowry, Christopher A., J.H. Hollis, A. De Vries, B. Pan, L.R. Brunet, J.R.F. Hunt, J.F.R. Paton et al. "Identification of an Immune-Responsive Mesolimbocortical Serotonergic System: Potential Role in Regulation of Emotional Behavior." *Neuroscience* 146, no. 2 (2007): 756–72.

Matthews, Dorothy, and Susan Jenks. "Can Bacteria Make You Smarter?" AAAS EurekAlert, May 24, 2010. https://www.eurekalert.org/pub_releases/2010-05/asfm-cbm052010.php.

McFarland, A.L., T.M. Waliczek, and J.M. Zajicek. "The Relationship between Student Use of Campus Green Spaces and Perceptions of Quality of Life." *HortTechnology* 18, no. 2 (2008): 232–38.

"Means Matter." Harvard T.H. Chan School of Public Health. Accessed February 13, 2018. https://www.hsph.harvard.edu/means-matter.

Meilman, Philip W., and Tanni M. Hall. "Aftermath of Tragic Events: The Development and Use of Community Support Meetings on a University Campus." *Journal of American College Health* 54, no. 6 (2006): 382–84.

Muir, John. *Our National Parks.* Boston: Houghton Mifflin, 1901.

Ogden, Cynthia L., Margaret D. Carroll, Hannah G. Lawman, Cheryl D. Fryar, Deanna Kruszon-Moran, Brian K. Kit, and Katherine M. Flegal. "Trends in Obesity Prevalence among Children and Adolescents in the United States, 1988–1994 through 2013–2014." *JAMA* 315, no. 21 (2016): 2292–99.

"The One Nature Challenge." David Suzuki Foundation. Accessed August 7, 2018. https://davidsuzuki.org/take-action/act-locally/one-nature-challenge/?nabe=5392362493968384:1&utm_referrer=https%3A%2F%2Fwww.google.com%2F.

Ottosson, Johan, and Patrik Grahn. "The Role of Natural Settings in Crisis Rehabilitation." *Landscape Restoration* 33 (2008): 51–70.

Outdoor Foundation. *Outdoor Recreation Report 2013.* https://outdoorindustry.org/wp-content/uploads/2017/05/2013-Outdoor-Research Participation1.pdf.

Park, Bum Jin, Yuko Tsunetsugu, Tamami Kasetani, Takahide Kagawa, and Yoshifumi Miyazaki. "The Physiological Effects of 'Shinrin-yoku' (Taking in the Forest Atmosphere or Forest Bathing): Evidence from Field Experiments in 24 Forests across Japan." *Environmental Health and Preventive Medicine* 15 (2010): 18–26.

Park Rx America. Accessed September 20, 2017. https://parkrxamerica.org/about.php.

Physical Activity Council. *2017 Participation Report: The Physical Activity Council's Annual Report Tracking Sports, Fitness, and Recreation Participation in the US.* 2017. http://physicalactivitycouncil.com/PDFs/current.pdf.

Prabhakararao, Sampathirao. "Overuse of Social Media Affects the Mental Health of Adolescents and Early Youth." *International Journal of Indian Psychiatry* 3, no. 2 (2016): 14–19.

Rhodes, Frank H.T. *The Creation of the Future: The Role of the American University.* Ithaca, NY: Cornell University Press, 2001.

Rideout, Victoria J., Ulla G. Foehr, and Donald F. Roberts. *Generation M2: Media in the Lives of 8- to 18-Year-Olds.* Menlo Park, CA: Henry J. Kaiser Family Foundation, 2010.

Schwartz, Allan J. "College Student Suicide in the United States: 1990–1991 through 2003–2004." *Journal of American College Health* 54, no. 6 (2006): 341–52.

Sheetz, Matthew J., and George L. King. "Molecular Understanding of Hyperglycemia's Adverse Effects for Diabetic Complications." *JAMA* 288 (2002): 2579–88.

Song, Chorong, Harumi Ikei, Miho Igarashi, Masayuki Miwa, Michiko Takagaki, and Yoshifumi Miyazaki. "Physiological and Psychological Responses of Young Males during Spring-Time Walks in Urban Parks." *Journal of Physiological Anthropology* 33, no. 1 (2014): 1–8.

Speake, Janet, Sally Edmondson, and Haq Nawaz. "Everyday Encounters with Nature: Students' Perceptions and Use of University Campus Green Spaces." *Human Geographies* 7, no. 1 (2013): 21–31.

Stigsdotter, Ulrika K., Anna Marie Palmsdottir, Ambra Burls, Alessandra Chermaz, Francesco Ferrini, and Patrik Grahn. "Nature-Based Therapeutic Interventions." In *Forest, Trees, and Human Health*, edited by Kjell Nilsson, Marcus Sangster, Christos Gallis, Terry Hartig, Sjerp de Vries, Klaus Seeland, and Jasper Schipperijn, chapter 11. Amsterdam: Springer Link, 2011.

Tennessen, Carolyn M., and Bernadine Cimprich. "Views of Nature: Effects on Attention." *Journal of Environmental Psychology* 15 (1995): 77–85.

Townsend, Mardie M., Cecily Pryor, and Anita Field. "Health and Well-Being Naturally: 'Contact with Nature' in Health Promotion for Targeted Individuals, Communities, and Populations." *Health Promotion Journal of Australia* 17, no. 2 (2006): 114–23.

Twenge, Jean M. *Generation Me: Why Today's Young Americans Are More Confident, Assertive, Entitled—and More Miserable Than Ever Before.* New York: Atria Paperback, 2014.

Ulrich, Roger S. "Human Responses to Vegetation and Landscapes." *Landscape and Urban Planning* 12 (1986): 29–44.

Ulrich, Roger S., Robert F. Simons, Barbara D. Losito, and Michael Zelson. "Stress Recovery during Exposure to Natural and Urban Environments." *Journal of Environmental Psychology* 11, no. 3 (1991): 201–30.

Van Den Berg, Agnes E., and Mariette H.G. Custers. "Gardening Promotes Neuroendocrine and Affective Restoration from Stress." *Journal of Health Psychology* 16, no. 1 (2011): 3–11.

Van den Berg, Agnes E., Marijke van Winsum-Westra, Sjerp de Vries, and Sonja M.E. van Dillen. "Allotment Gardening and Health: A Comparative Survey among Allotment Gardeners and Their Neighbors without an Allotment." *Environmental Health* 9 (2010): 74.

Wassenberg, Christopher L., Marni A. Goldenberg, and Katherine E. Soule. "Benefits of Botanical Garden Visitation: A Means-End Study." *Urban Forestry and Urban Greening* 14 (2015): 148–55.

Whitlock, Janis. "Self-Injurious Behavior in Adolescents." *PLoS Med* 7 no. 5 (2010): e1000240. https://doi.org/10.1371/journal.pmed.1000240.

Zarr, Robert, Linda Cottrell, and Chaya Merrill. "Park Prescription (DC Park Rx): A New Strategy to Combat Chronic Disease in Children." *Journal of Physical Activity and Health* 14 (2017): 1–2.

Index

31901065169254